Designed to Shine

Designed to Shine

LIVING INTENTIONALLY TO DISCOVER YOUR INNER *Light*

KRISTIN SVETS

gatekeeper press
Tampa, Florida

The views and opinions expressed in this book are solely those of the author and do not necessarily reflect the views or opinions of Gatekeeper Press. Gatekeeper Press is not to be held responsible for and expressly disclaims responsibility of the content herein.

DESIGNED TO SHINE:
Live Intentionally to Discover Your Inner Light

Published by Gatekeeper Press
2167 Stringtown Rd, Suite 109
Columbus, OH 43123-2989
www.GatekeeperPress.com

Copyright © 2023 by Kristin Svets

All rights reserved. Neither this book, nor any parts within it may be sold or reproduced in any form or by any electronic or mechanical means, including information storage and retrieval systems, without permission in writing from the author. The only exception is by a reviewer, who may quote short excerpts in a review.

The author of this book is not offering medical or mental health advice as the author is not a licensed medical or mental health professional. The techniques in this book are not a form of treatment for medical, emotional, or psychological issues, and you should seek professional advice if your situation warrants that. The intent of the author is to offer information and motivation of a general nature on a personal development path. In the event you use any of the information in this book for yourself, the author assumes no responsibility for your actions and disclaims any liability, loss, or damages which is incurred as a consequence, directly or indirectly, of the use and application of any of the contents of this book.

Library of Congress Control Number: 2022938524

ISBN (paperback): 9781662923524
eISBN: 9781662923531

CONTENTS

INTRODUCTION: Out of Your Head and into Your Heart: A Future Self Vision   1

PART 1: Grounded in Loving Kindness—the Embodiment   11

1. The Power of Grounding   15
2. The Magic of Meditation and Breathwork   24
3. The Attitude of Gratitude   35
4. The Wisdom of Journaling   49

PART 2: Centered in Harmony—the Empowerment   57

5. Being Mindful of Your Mindset   60
6. Rediscover the Authentic You   67
7. Awaken Your Strengths and Values   73
8. Be the Peacekeeper of Your Heart and Soul   85
9. Embracing Harmony and Duality   103

PART 3: Uplifted by Light—the Enlightenment   117

10. The Light around Us   121
11. The Light within Us   127
12. Honoring Your Season of Life   136
13. Choosing Joy   147
14. Shine in Your Soulful Vision   157
15. Abundance Is Success of the Soul   163

PART 4: Poems, Affirmations, and Musings from My Heart   177

DEDICATION   190

REFERENCES   191

INTRODUCTION

Out of Your Head and into Your Heart: A Future Self Vision

I always thought I needed a permission slip to go bigger. Or maybe I was waiting for that invitation to show up, shine brighter, and share more of myself with the world.

I truly believed that someone else would see my gifts and say, "Yes, you are amazing! You should write a book! You should start a podcast! You should speak to our group! You should coach and teach people!"

And while a few lovely comments were sent my way over time, that beautiful, heavy, glossy, three-piece paper invitation that I was waiting for never showed up.

As my fiftieth birthday started to get closer, as that middle-season-of-life wisdom started to kick in, it finally hit me. I realized the only person that I needed a permission slip from was myself. The invitation from the universe was already there.

It was time to get out of my head and into my heart.

So, I did just that.

I created a vision of the future version of me, and I saw her every day. We had a little dance party before I would sit down to write.

She was a published author. She wore a green suit at her book signing. She was confident, proud, peaceful, fulfilled, full of joy.

DESIGNED TO SHINE

She would share her story of figuring out what it meant to become grounded, discovering the gifts of harmony, and using heart-centered practices to find a deeper fulfillment and joy in this amazing journey of life.

She would be sharing her story of deciding to shine.

I created this vision, a little bit at a time.

That green suit literally came to me in a dream, all on its own. I didn't know why I had dreamt of a suit in a color that wasn't already a staple part of my wardrobe.

And then the vision of me wearing that suit at my book signing came to me in a meditation. I loved that vision. And I knew it was going to happen as soon as I saw it.

The fact that this dream of the suit was so specific was not lost on me, so I decided to research the meaning of green. Green is the color of growth, renewal, energy, and nature. In a spiritual context, green can represent a balance between the body and mind. It represents harmony, which is not only my greatest strength but was already a major part of the structure of this future book. In yoga, green represents the heart chakra, which is also the center for peace, compassion, kindness, and love. The symbolism of that color coming to me and the message I was wanting to share through this book was not coincidental. It was a gift from my inner wisdom, from the universe, from creation.

That's the power of slowing down and opening up your heart so that you can tap into your own inner wisdom. You can find that light inside of you and let it shine. You can choose to create your future vision of yourself.

INTRODUCTION

Of course, I did have my moments on this journey.

The noisy inner critic in my head was plenty loud.

I heard that voice saying things like, "You don't have anything to share that hasn't been said before. There are such better versions that already exist." Or, "Who are you to think you can do this?" And, "There are people out there who have such a greater impact than you. Just let them do the talking. You don't need to say anything. Just stop." There were many more iterations of this inner saboteur's message.

While that voice was definitely successful in allowing me to drag my feet, sometimes for weeks that turned into months at a time, how exactly did I overcome it to actually finish this book in order to manifest that book signing vision of myself in the green suit?

It took some deep reflection and healing about what was holding me back. While hitting rock bottom was luckily never a part of my journey, recognizing and releasing the big and little traumas along the path of life was a requirement. Whenever I have witnessed and experienced challenges in life, my gift was realizing that there was a better way of perceiving things and a more empowering way of acting and being, which I share throughout the book. This process also required looking at these life experiences that I had emotionally pushed down and allowing the space in my body, mind, and soul to be free of the stories that no longer served me. Equally impactful, the book-writing process forced me to open up and embrace the parts of me that wanted to be shared, that wanted to shine.

I got out of my head and into my heart. I acknowledged that voice of fear and doubt. I know it was trying to protect me and keep me safe. I got into the heart-centered habit of thanking it for still being there and doing its job. The conversation in my head would unfold in that I would let that voice of fear know that I had a bigger job to do. That my version of inspiration counts. And that if my words and message help only a few people, that is still of important service. I also wanted to do this to show myself that I could. It was time to let my heart lead, although the mind was a welcome companion, keeping us safe on the ride.

It was part of my journey. It was part of my purpose. It was a part of my story.

So, what do I want you, my reader, to know and take from this?

Life is not a dress rehearsal.

This is it.

We can give ourselves that permission slip to tap into the heart-centered inspiration within ourselves and create what we want.

The invitation already exists. The world wants us all to show up. That's why we are here.

We can approach life with a calm determination and a centered persistence that is filled with both peace and strength, wisdom and courage.

We can find inner harmony and be more connected to our soulful vision.

We only have to take the leap and dive in.

INTRODUCTION

You are truly designed to shine.

You might have forgotten this in the busyness of your everyday life.

You might have forgotten this because your inner critic says it's not true.

Or you might actually believe it, but you hesitate to go all in, because you lack clarity about even knowing what you want.

This is where the intention to create the design of your life comes in.

Just like planning a great vacation, celebration, or dream home, it takes the vision and the action to bring the dream into its full light.

The steps to shining your light and living in alignment with your soulful vision of your life are only possible through intention and integration.

Alignment, Integration, Mindset: A.I.M. for your soulful vision. This is the cornerstone of the work that I do with my clients. It is the cornerstone of the work that I do on myself. And it is the cornerstone of this book and will show up as repeating themes in each section. These are the pillars of deciding to believe that you are designed to shine.

Your corner of the world needs your light.

You are the one that has to decide to turn it on.

You hold your own permission slip.

You can accept the invitation.

You can let your heart lead.

DESIGNED TO SHINE

You can let your radiance come through.

You might be waiting until the time is right. Maybe you aren't ready to show up differently or practice mindfulness because things seem too chaotic right now. Here's the thing: the world is always going to throw chaos our way. We can look at history to see that chaos has always been a part of the human experience. We get complacent or comfortable when things are going well, and we get into a space with the illusion that we don't need these practices. And then we get to this flip side, where we also put off these practices in stressful times thinking that we will do it when things slow down.

"When things are calmer, I will find more time for a gratitude practice."

"I will try meditation again when I have more time, but things are too hectic right now."

This is the fallacy. Things are not going to slow down unless *you* slow them down. You decide and create the space to make this personal growth happen. You create the space for inner peace. You create the space to be the calm in the chaos. You create the space to shine your light.

If I had to choose a core message to share with you, it's that you are inherently worthy. You are enough. You are light. You are designed to shine. And you have to be proactive!

If you'd like to hear more about why I believe that about you, and how to tap into that belief for yourself, then read on. I share my perspectives, learnings, and practices for living in these beliefs. I've

INTRODUCTION

also included some poems that came from my heart. It's really my journey and the work that I have done to get to this place, writing a book, and deciding to shine. I hope this work serves you and encourages you to also drop out of your head and into your heart.

I also believe that a part of my calling is to connect the spiritual practices with our everyday life. My goal is to take what some view as "woo-woo" or nonsense and make it real and accessible to everyone. This personal development path has two parts to it that go hand in hand throughout the journey: self-awareness in the here and now, and the growth and connection to your soulful vision. This is being intentional to be grounded and embodied, centered and empowered, and uplifted and enlightened.

I've included integration practices at the end of each chapter, because while words can teach and inspire, that is just cognitive learning. If you don't integrate and implement the daily or regular practices and actually embody them, it will be difficult to create real change. I know this from experience. The practices are the discovery tools. The practices integrate the growth. The practices are the path to embodying and radiating your light.

I invite you to view this book as a way to cultivate heart-centered harmony in your body, mind, and soul. The book is split into three sections that somewhat coincide with those three: body (grounded), mind (centered), and soul (uplifted). There are overlapping messages and integrations between them, because they all work in unison.

DESIGNED TO SHINE

I hope this book sparks that light within you to listen to your heart and make your world a little brighter.

Let your light shine, my friends. There is no time like the present. It's all we have.

In gratitude,

Kristin

(Note: I am not a therapist or a doctor, so I am not giving medical or mental health advice. Nothing in this book should be taken as medical or mental health advice. I am sharing my perspectives and practices as to what has worked for me for finding more fulfillment and connection in my normal life with everyday problems, which hopefully serves you. Always check with your doctor or therapist to determine if you have questions about whether or not something is right for you, or if you are triggered by any of my stories. Mental health issues are very different from tapping into everyday motivation and new perspectives. This book discusses thought reframing and spiritual exploration, and my intention here is not one of toxic positivity nor of spiritual bypassing. Rather, it is one of empowerment for those not suffering from mental health issues. Please do not use this book as advice for mental health issues; if you need care, seek mental health care from a professional. My intention is for this to be supportive and offer new perspectives. Sending love to all of you!)

PART ONE

Grounded in Loving Kindness—the Embodiment

DESIGNED TO SHINE

The Ripple Effect: A Poem

I started as a stream,
A small little stream at first.
And then I slowly started to grow.
Sometimes I would rush
And then realize I could slow down.
But I was always flowing.
I had patience.
I had the power of consistency.
I had the power of time.
I expanded to a river:
Moving faster when I was called to,
Slowing down when I needed to.
But I was always flowing.
I was pretty happy with what a beautiful river I became.
I didn't realize for a very long time that it's not just the water itself that holds my beauty.
It's beyond that.
It's beyond the current riverbank.

I was always flowing,
Not realizing the vastness of the beauty of my creation.
Not aware of how my existence had such a great impact on my surroundings.
I'm not just the beauty of the water flowing.
I've created beauty far beyond the edges of my flowing water.
I created the grandest, most awe-inspiring creation through rock—
Through glorious, colorful rock.
Have you seen what I made?
The Grand Canyon.

PART ONE

Can you believe I actually did that?
Can you imagine if I had stopped flowing?
I didn't even know I was doing it.

I am more than a stream, more than a river.
I am the river of life.
I am the Ripple Effect.
You started as a stream too—and now you are a river.
You are creating your own vastness of beauty,
Your own Grand Canyon.
And you don't even realize it.
You are just doing your thing.
You are just flowing along:
Hustling when it's called for,
Resting when you need to.
And what a gift that is.
Your impact is so much more than you can see.
Your power resonates beyond the edges of you.
The beauty that you bring to your environment is so much greater than you know.
You are the river.
You are the river of life.
You are the Ripple Effect.

Believe it.
Keep flowing.
Be patient.
Keep flowing.
Be consistent.

. 13 .

DESIGNED TO SHINE

Keep flowing.
Be here now.
And keep flowing.

The beauty is unfolding.
The beauty is in the creation.
The beauty is within you.
The beauty is overflowing from you.
The beauty is vast.
The beauty is you.
The beauty is the river.
The beauty is the river of life.
The beauty is the Ripple Effect.
You are unfolding.
You are the creation.
You are overflowing.
You are vast.
You are the river.
You are the river of life.
You are the Ripple Effect.

1
The Power of Grounding

Why would anyone start an excursion at 2:00 a.m., in a van, to ride for hours up to the top of a volcano and stand in the dark night sky and freezing cold with whipping winds?

To see the magic of a sunrise over Mount Haleakalā in Hawaii.

My husband and I did this on our honeymoon. And while we were still technically on the earth, it felt as if we were almost touching the dark night sky and the beautiful stars within it.

Just when you think you cannot take the wind and cold any longer, and your nose and fingers are numb, and you are shivering too much to drink your warm coffee, the dark night sky slowly starts to shift.

The beautiful shades of pink and orange start so softly and become brighter and brighter. And then you see it. The first sliver of the sun.

It's like watching all the shapes of the moon cycle, but in just a few short minutes. The sliver on the horizon becomes a quarter of the circle, then half, then three-quarters ...

And then there it is. The full sun in its morning glory.

Strangers cry and laugh and cheer together at the beauty.

It's stunning.

Why does this move us? Why is our emotion stirred with a sunrise or a sunset?

Because it shows us the power of nature, the vastness and the power of the universe.

It reminds us of what we know to be true: that we are a part of something so much bigger than ourselves.

And when we witness it, it resonates in our core.

The emotion is our body's response to that inner knowledge.

We recognize the amazing beauty of what we are witnessing, of what we belong to.

And while that happened on what felt like a journey far above the earth, it is the essence and the power of *grounding*.

But what exactly is grounding? There are many ways to interpret and define it. What resonates with me is that it is recreating the connection between nature and our body. It is heightening the awareness of being a part of nature, and it is heightening your awareness of connection to the universe and higher power and bringing that into your body. It is being present in the moment to feel the richness of this experience of life.

You can see other examples of this in so many places. The cheers and applause in Key West at the daily sunset. The emotion shown by experienced weathermen when witnessing a solar eclipse. Even when we are alone, cheers and applause erupt inside of us when we witness the beauty of nature, whether it is from a mountaintop or an ocean beach or any other favorite spot in nature that makes our hearts sing.

However, you definitely do not need a special trip or moment to experience grounding. These are very grand examples of ground-

PART ONE

ing, but it can be just as profound in the simple things. Grounding practices can easily become a part of your daily life, and they can cost you nothing.

The basic premise of grounding is to stand barefoot outside so that your feet can touch and feel the ground. We know in our core that this feels good most of the time. And the fact that we live our modern lives so disconnected from nature makes it somewhat of a novelty to do this. Studies have been done on the potential benefits of the electrons on the surface of the earth and how direct contact may benefit human health. (I am not a scientist or an official researcher, but a quick Internet search will show you multiple studies.) What I know is that it feels good, especially, in my case, if it is warm sand!

Do you have any childhood memories that recall clearly your connection to nature? When I was very young, we used to play hide-and-seek in a cornfield (before the horror movie made that seem insane). I can clearly remember the dirt on the ground, the size of the cornstalks, and the sunlight coming through the rows. I can see what the stalks looked like, felt like, smelled like, and how they were incredible at hiding us! I have another memory that includes my sister and two of our cousins, engaging in our favorite activity of climbing up a small gorge of steep beautiful rocks and a delightful flowing little stream. I can feel the water and rocks on my feet. I can hear the stream splashing and the rustle of the wind on the leaves in the trees around us. I can smell the greenery that surrounds us. I can hear us yelling and laughing and losing our breath as we race to the top and then back down.

Those connections of being fully present in nature and fully present in the moment stick with us because they nourish our entire well-being. Those moments connect us to our inner peace. They allow us to experience being a part of something bigger, the purpose of which at that moment is our enjoyment. It's beautiful. It's grounding. It's centering. It's the experience of those little life moments that are really the big life moments.

There is an entire practice called "forest bathing" that has become incredibly popular due to how good it can make you feel. The term *Shinrin-yoku* (which translates as "forest bathing") was originally coined in Japan by Qing Li, MD, in the 1980s as an anecdote to the hustle and indoor lifestyle that was causing an increase in mental, emotional, and physical health issues. Japan adopted it as a part of their national health program because it was so effective and beneficial. We have also seen this become a part of the private mental health programs in the United States, as so many of them are located in places where there is plenty of sunshine and access to the outdoors.

So how do we take advantage of this powerful ideology? We want to proactively create more of those moments to connect back to ourselves, to nature, and to the present. This can be done through any scenario in which you can tap into several or all of your five senses, enriching your experience of the present moment. There is the literal practice of being in nature and feeling the ground beneath your feet, taking off your socks and shoes and feeling the grass, the dirt, the sand; whatever version of the actual ground that

PART ONE

you have access to feel. It can mean touching a tree, smelling the flowers, stacking rocks, or rubbing rock crystals in the palms of your hands. It could be as simple as rubbing your hands together to create warmth and energy. It can be lighting the candle in your home or watching the rain or snow through your window. That's still connecting with nature. There is no right or wrong way to ground yourself.

Breathwork and meditation are both incredibly powerful grounding mindfulness practices as well, which we will dive deeper into exploring shortly.

But first, let's discuss why we want to tap into the power of grounding and incorporate it into our lives. What is the point?

Being present in the moment is a gift, and grounding creates a heightened awareness in the present. This helps us remember to tap back into who we are underneath the layers of our created lives. Truly, the present moment is the only thing we ever really have. When we get to the next moment, the future is still ahead of us, out there on the horizon. We can only actually experience the now. And what do we want that to be? When we train our brains to more fully experience this present moment, then we can see how we can create the experiences that we want to be having. We are anchoring into the present moment. This is the first step to creating alignment in our lives.

Another reason that grounding and becoming more aware of who we are right now is that our bodies are always processing the feelings that are associated with our subconscious thoughts. That's why we feel that neck and shoulder pain when we are stressed out. That's why we can get butterflies in our stomach when we are nervous. That's why our heart rate increases when we are scared. Many studies show that reducing stress can also reduce a plethora of physical ailments. When we can anchor in our new awareness and renewed desire for inner peace and growth, any stress reduction activities like these grounding practices will work so much more deeply.

We need to embody these practices to help us shift and actually create those changes in both our body and our mindset, which then leads to new actions in our lives. In the same way that our body is holding on to and processing our negative subconscious thoughts, we need to create new feelings in our bodies. We can use our conscious, empowering thoughts to add in more grounding practices, which we will then feel in our bodies, creating more awareness and richness in the present. We must create the new feelings in our bodies. We are being proactive to regulate our nervous system. This is integration, and this is intentional living.

You will often hear people talk about manifestation and that you have to be in the energy of that future thing that you want. This is a difficult concept to grasp when you are first introduced to it. Many athletes are taught to use visualization as a part of their practice and to help them get ready for big competitions. Actors go through the rehearsal process for their projects. We want to do that same thing for our soulful life vision, but we will often hit some roadblocks and limiting beliefs that we have to work through. The

PART ONE

various grounding practices in this chapter and the awareness of feelings in your body will help you move through these obstacles and bring that envisioned energy into the current moment and your current state.

The visualization technique that I shared in the introduction can be viewed as a grounding technique, even though it was future-focused. By visualizing how I wanted the future me to feel, the one who had completed this book and was at her book signing, I brought that feeling into the everyday moment to tap into the motivation to write. It had to be a feeling in the present moment. I had to choose to create the future from the here and now. I had to embody that feeling.

Gaining insight into who we are now and who we want to be is the only way to create lasting change in our being. And we must choose to be that new version now, in the present. It is how we bring alignment, integration, and mindset all together.

Have you ever tapped into your willpower and accomplished something that felt really great, like eating healthy and eliminating sugar for thirty days? Or maybe it was completing a sixty-day fitness regimen. And you are so proud of yourself when you complete it, and you love how you feel, and yet you don't stick to it? You slowly creep back into your old ways? It happens to the best of us! This is the ongoing complexity of working with our brain that is trying to keep us safe and comfortable. When you have trained your brain to be more aware and more present through grounding practices, you will have a stronger capacity to make the choices that you want to make and to stick with them.

Commitment is always in the moment. It's always in the now. The more you practice being present, the stronger your ability will be to follow through on whatever you are committed to creating in your life. This strengthens your resilience, and it is the foundation of intentional living.

You can choose to feel more grounded. You can choose to feel calmer. You can choose to make decisions by checking with your head and your heart. You always have that power. Grounding will strengthen your mind and well-being. *Calmness of the mind* is one of the beautiful tools of wisdom that will grant you access to your inner peace and centered determination to stick to commitments and bring visions to life.

Integration: How to Do a Five-Senses Mindfulness Practice

This is your invitation to use the principles of forest bathing. This is the process of using all five senses to enrich the experience of your time in the forest. You can do this same process with any experience, such as a simple food or drink. Use your senses to become grounded in the present moment. You can ask yourself the following questions: What do you smell? What do you feel? What do you see? What do you hear? What do you taste? Do this slowly. Witness your full sensory experience of it. This allows you to train your brain to really savor the moment.

PART ONE

Take a silent nature walk. Go barefoot if it's sand or grass or another comfortable surface. Connect to the ground. Connect to the nature around you and let it nourish you. Feel the support. Feel the air on your skin. See the beauty in the little things and big things around you. Notice their textures. Smell the air. Hear the birds or the wind or the waves or the rain. Run through your sensations of the moment. Be fully present. Let it fill your soul.

Whenever you want to use a grounding practice to become more present in your daily life, begin to ask yourself these impactful questions: Who am I being in this moment? Is it in alignment with who I want to be in this moment? How can I make a slight shift to be closer to who I want to be right now?

Being grounded and aware enriches our experiences. The rewards of enriching your own experience and that of others are immeasurable, as it truly connects you to your inner peace and connects you to your soul. Fulfillment, happiness, and joy live in these spaces.

When you feel grounded and centered, you are training yourself to be calm in the chaos. You are learning to listen to your heart. You are living intentionally and training yourself that you can shine your light.

Two of my favorite grounding practices that are accessible to you right now are meditation and breathwork. They have been such life-enhancing tools for me. Let's dive into those.

2
The Magic of Meditation and Breathwork

"Wow, this feels like forever!" "Oh my goodness, I am so bad at meditation." "When is this over? Can I open my eyes yet? Are we done?" "What is this weirdness all about?"

Have you heard these things in your mind when you've tried meditating, or even when you've thought about it? Yes, I know; I heard them too. If you have tried it before and told yourself that you are bad at it and that it wasn't for you, consider giving it a few more tries and letting go of the self-criticism. This chapter will help you learn how to do that.

Here are two fun juxtapositions about meditation and breathwork:

1. By choosing to slow down and be still, you are being proactive!

2. You are not doing meditation and breathwork just for the experience in the moment (which can be lovely in and of itself but doesn't always feel good). You are doing it for the benefits that flow out into the rest of your life. This is a key mindset shift to embrace!

PART ONE

When I first sat in meditation, my mind would race and I experienced the common judgmental thoughts that I was bad at it. I thought this "sitting still" probably wasn't for me. When I first sat in a yoga class and the instructor had everyone hum "Om" in unison, I was incredibly uncomfortable and sat in my secluded place of judgment ("this is so weird!"). But something always called me back. I knew there was something more to this. And the small exposures over time, combined with my fascination with the research behind the benefits of meditation, started to intrigue me. And then, it spoke to me in a distinct message from my heart, or my mind's eye, or my intuition. Maybe it was all of them speaking together. But it was clear.

"You need to teach this to people. You need to share it." The first time I really felt like meditation was something I could do, something I could grasp, no longer something I was bad at, I heard this message from my inner wisdom while I was meditating. This was an absurd idea to me at my ego level at the time, because I was not in any capacity a yoga teacher or a meditation teacher or even a coach. How would I teach this? Who would listen to me? But the inner knowledge spoke back: "You don't have to know right now. Just know that it's going to be." And I did. I knew it was true. I released the "how" but had faith in the vision. It's taken about three years from the time I heard that message, and I have been trusting the process.

This is just one example that I have experienced of tapping into my inner knowledge through meditation. Another example I love was that for a period of time, I ran a makeup artistry business, and the name "Abundant Beauty" was a name that came to me in meditation. This name has a significantly spiritual vibe for a makeup business (which was a nod as to where I was headed). Another insight that I mentioned in the introduction of this book, the vision of me in my green suit at my own book signing, was crystal clear to me in a meditation. When making decisions about a variety of things, I use meditation as the best place for me to check in with myself to see if it's really aligned with who I want to be in that season of my life.

This is the power of slowing down, pausing your body and mind, and tuning in. This is the power of meditation: the awareness, the insights, the inner knowledge, the peace.

Do you experience your great ideas in the shower or in the middle of the night? That is a similar scenario in which you have given your mind a moment of peace to allow creativity to flow.

While inner peace and greater clarity in life sound nice, I realize that is not motivating enough on the front end for most people. Did you know that many of the biggest issues you may be experiencing might be helped by meditation? What if it helped you reduce stress? Improve your sleep habits? What if you could assist your own nervous system?

Let's talk science! The research on meditation is astounding and motivating. Several studies have shown an array of amazing health benefits, indicating that a regular meditation practice could improve sleep, reduce anxiety, lower stress, increase resiliency,

PART ONE

assist in pain management, improve immune function, improve cardiovascular health, prevent cognitive decline with aging, and more. *(REFERENCE 1: Various Studies on Meditation and Potential Health Benefits)*

Other studies have shown that within minutes of meditating, dopamine and other "happy" hormones are released into our bodies, providing a feeling of calm and relaxation. Dopamine has also been shown to be the chemical that you need for motivation! When you are trying to accomplish a bigger or more aligned vision for yourself, you need dopamine on your side, and meditation may help increase your dopamine. *(REFERENCE 2: A Study on Meditation and Dopamine Release)* There are countless books and texts that dive deeply into these topics. (If it interests you to research this further, this information is readily available from a quick Internet search.)

I truly believe meditation is the ultimate self-care tool. Not only is it backed by research as an effective tool physically, but it is also our pathway to inner peace. It is our pathway to being grounded as well as to envision a soul-fulfilling future. It is the path to nourishment and service. It is the path to shining our light and stepping into our power. It was my pathway to writing this book.

There are so many different versions of meditation. Trying them is the best way to see what speaks to you, and know that there are other types to try if you don't get anything out of one type. Keep researching. There are guided meditations, mantra meditations, music meditations, silent meditations, transcendental meditation, and more. I personally like to use different ones on different days. There are so many apps out there that make it so easy. At the end of this chapter, there is a framework on how to do a basic meditation practice on your own.

If you are encountering some resistance to the idea of meditation, consider trying to set aside five to ten minutes for silence. You don't have to do anything. You don't have to release your thoughts or focus on anything. You just commit to sitting in silence. This is a great practice for those of you who don't want to meditate, as it will still nourish you with a mindful pause. Maybe it's sitting outside in the fresh air in silence. Similar to the space you give yourself for those few minutes in the shower for new ideas to come your way, this is a step to being proactive about allowing some space to pause.

Meditation was an alignment piece of the puzzle for me, giving me that grounded, centered presence and creating more awareness. It integrated the mindset work. The proactive commitment to the practice itself was a new daily integration. And this allowed for my inner wisdom and inner knowledge to be honored and heard.

What I realized when I was introduced to breathwork was that I could create an even deeper implementation and integration into the rest of my life. Yes, my meditation practice had created incredible change. But I wanted to embody and expand these changes further. For me, combining meditation with breathwork took everything to that next level.

PART ONE

What is Breathwork, and Why Use It?

Think of a moment when you have intuitively used deep breaths to calm yourself down, maybe before a test or big meeting or important conversation. This is your body's ability to know the truth of what you need in that scenario.

While your body is holding onto stress and emotions, it is also holding onto innate wisdom. Wouldn't it be great to strengthen your ability to use that wisdom more frequently? Wouldn't it be great to know how to use your breath to manipulate your nervous system to work for you and invite in stress reduction?

Breathwork is a range of practices and techniques that encompass intentionally controlling and manipulating your breath in a variety of ways with multiple purposes, such as creating a sense of calm or a renewed energy level. It is such an amazing tool to get you centered and grounded into your body right away. Everyone could benefit from gentle breathwork, and most of us can benefit from advanced techniques. Incorporating breathwork into my routine took me to the next level of embodying who I needed to be in the present to bring my soulful vision to life. And I knew I needed to learn how to teach this along with meditation, as it would take my coaching clients further into their transformations, as it had mine. Even if you have thought you were bad at meditation, or if you have never tried it, you have been breathing your whole life. You know the life-giving power of your breath. Intentionally using your breath as an ally to create the change that you cognitively want to make is an incredible thing to learn to do.

I spent over a year in various life coach training programs. The process was an incredible journey in growth and awareness. One of my personal greatest challenges was that even with the new awareness and realization of how I could live a more aligned life with my values, I was still getting stuck in the follow-through and implementation of the ways I wanted to elevate my life. This wasn't due to a fault in the program or in my coaches or peer coaches. It was about the depth to which I had created agreements with my limiting beliefs at a subconscious level. The new awareness created the realization that I had to tap into my own inner coach to stay in that energy and integrate the desire to make changes as frequently as possible. The awareness of my own internal resistance to actually follow through and create the change I cognitively wanted to make was eye-opening. This wasn't just a mindset reframe; this was going to require releasing the subconscious stuck energy in my body that was holding me back.

This feeling of being stuck is the same thing that so many of us deal with when we face the inability to stick to a workout routine or healthier eating for the long term. This resistance is due to the fact that our brain has to be rewired to release different chemicals, moving from stress-related cortisol to relaxation-inducing dopamine. It is about creating space and safety in our body for these changes. As I moved through this, I was much more aware of how I wanted to change, but I needed a physical practice that pulled in my mindset to make it actually happen by breaking through those subconscious habits, beliefs, and agreements. I had to change my

PART ONE

habitual chemical body's state and reaction to my daily life. Breathwork gave me the tools to embody the release and embody the change. It allowed me to tap into my body, release more "happiness" chemicals, and intentionally move forward to create those changes. And it deepened my meditation practice. This was the missing link of how I wanted to teach meditation, and I now prefer them as a combined practice. Breathwork is the deepening of the integration.

Here's a fascinating aspect of breathwork to think about: our breath is the only voluntary and involuntary physiological action of the body and brain. We all know the power of deep, slow breaths when we are stressed out. When we truly harness this power of breath, we can intentionally turn on our own internal stress relief system. There are breathwork practices for a variety of intentions, such as calming, balancing, and energizing practices. We can create a breathwork sequence with the intention to tap into your creativity and intuition or one with the intention to tap into your confidence and power. We can create a breathwork practice with the intention to reduce stress and improve sleep or to improve how you show up as a leader. The intentions behind the practice are unlimited.

Breathwork itself is an incredible combination of expansion and embodiment.

What I love about starting a breathwork practice for someone who is new or hesitant to practice meditation is that breathwork keeps your brain busy and inherently allows you to be present in the moment. For those of you who have tried meditation and claimed to be bad at it because your brain is running, you might really feel more successful with a breathwork practice. (Let me interject here that these adjectives of *good* or *bad, successful* or *unsuccessful* are not a mindful way to reflect upon these practices, but I know that all of our judging brains like these labels. I challenge you to reframe your thoughts about what it should be and just allow it to be as it is.)

When you are manipulating your breath and counting your breath patterns, your brain is occupied and present. The mantra "Be Here Now" is so much easier to comprehend and implement after a breathwork session. And the gift of that experience is that breathwork is also an amazing gateway to being centered in your body for a deeper meditation. Breathwork and meditation go hand in hand. They are your zen-inducing best friends.

Another great aspect of learning breathwork techniques is that you can use them to become more grounded and present at any moment of your life. It's accessible when you are driving your car or sitting at your desk. It's accessible when you can't sleep. It's accessible when you are stressed out. Just a few deep slow inhales and exhales can release so much stuck energy. It can help you just be.

In my experience, the combination of breathwork and meditation is the fastest and deepest way to alignment, integration, and mindset cohesiveness. An extra nourishing step that I love to add is putting one or both hands on your heart. It feels so nourishing. It will open the doors to your inner peace and soulful vision. It will make your heart glow. It is a retreat for your soul.

PART ONE

If you would like to look at some of the studies that show the potential benefits of breathwork, a few of them are noted at the back of this book. *(REFERENCE 3: Various Studies on Breathwork Practices and Potential Benefits)*

Integration: How to Do a Basic Breathwork and Meditation Practice

Supplies needed: Nothing is required! You have all you need.

Nice extras: A blanket or small pillow to sit on, a candle or essential oils, meditation music or a recording of a guided meditation (although silence is wonderful too).

Steps: Start by sitting upright, comfortable but strong and alert. Think of elongating the back of your neck, relaxing your shoulders, and opening your heart. Relax your jaw, close your eyes, and place your hands on your thighs, with your palms facing up (to receive) or down (to ground). Begin by focusing on the sound of your breath, and start the breathwork part by taking three deep, long, cleansing inhales and exhales, breathing in through your nose and out through your mouth. Seal your lips for equal ratio breathing, or box breath, which will all be done in and out of your nose. Inhale for a count of five, hold for five, exhale for five, and hold at the bottom for five. Repeat this breath pattern for three rotations, allowing the sense of balance and grounding to center you. Returning to your natural breathing and start to do a body scan, beginning with your toes and feet and then focusing your attention up through each section of your body. Become aware of the ground supporting you and how your body is holding space for you. Don't judge your thoughts as they start to wander. See them as clouds passing by in the sky. You may use a mantra, or a sound like "Om," or an affirmation to help focus the mind and create an intention. And just be. Sit for as long as you like. (Five to ten minutes is a great starting point for new meditators.)

Journaling is a great action after a meditation practice as you may have thoughts and ideas that come to you that you want to jot down. We'll go more into the power of journaling later in the book.

You are worthy of taking the time to experience the present moment.

Listen to the wisdom of your heart, and light up your world.

You are designed to shine.

One of the most powerful ways to be grounded in the present moment and to ignite that inner light is to adopt an attitude of gratitude.

3
The Attitude of Gratitude

Sometimes strangers are actually angels dropping messages as they pass you by, a little shooting star. A soft form of grief was my current companion as I was sitting with my two- and four-year-old boys at a new park, as we had just moved across the country. I was feeling so alone, desperately missing all the family, friends, community, and connections we had left behind. And as I was sitting with my sadness and loneliness, wiping toddlers' dirty hands and digging out snacks, a tall older gentleman walked by and said, "What wonderful little companions you have right there." And he kept walking. Those words hit me in my soul. Yes, there were wonderful, beautiful little companions right in front of me. I wasn't alone at all. I actually had so much beauty with me in these sweet little ones. It brought tears to my eyes. I think about that man and those words in that moment all of the time, years and years later. It was so simple, and exactly what I needed to hear. What a gift, what a reminder, what a message from an angel. What a shooting star.

This is the power of choosing your thoughts and reframing how you respond to what is happening in your life. That's the power of choosing gratitude in the moment. And I don't mean to bypass the validity of my sadness at that moment. It was warranted, as I was feeling alone after a big move. But the way to move through that sadness is to simultaneously look for what is good in the moment. And what was good was my beautiful little companions.

I had an extended version of a famous Charles Swindoll quote about how attitude is the most impactful part of the experience of life. I had it posted in my cubicle for the almost ten years that I worked in corporate banking. While the environment of my cubicle was the typical gray fabric used in many offices, which some would see as a potentially depressing little square, I never had a problem with my space. Did I focus on the size or color or lack of privacy? No, I did not. Do you think the reminder from the attitude quote helped me frame my thoughts about that environment? Absolutely. I actually think that quote has defined much of my adult life with its power of repetition in my psyche on a daily basis for almost a decade.

Reframing your thoughts is the premise behind a gratitude practice and training our minds to see the good. We choose how we interpret things and how we allow those things to make us feel. We always have the power to choose new thoughts and create new feelings. Our attitude toward every part of our lives directly affects our perception and then our reality of it. One of the most impactful places to learn to create that more positive attitude is with a gratitude practice.

Gratitude, to me, is where everything starts and everything ends. Gratitude is the foundation for a happier life. It is also the foundation for growth. Gratitude is both a part of being grounded and a part of being able to shine your light from a place of love and service, not ego and attention. The attitude of gratitude is our saving grace and is a direct path to feeling fulfilled and content in our lives.

PART ONE

I've noticed with my clients, and even with myself, that gratitude can have many types of stories that come with it. Something that has been helpful for me is to play with different versions of the wording, such as thankfulness and appreciation. They each have their own nuance, so see which feels the lightest to you.

Sometimes we may struggle with gratitude because there is an underlying message of guilt that can be associated with it. "I am grateful for this food because I could go hungry." "I am grateful for my home because I could be homeless." In order to release the undertone of assuming that you "should" feel a certain way, see how it feels to use another similar word. "I am thankful for my home." Does it reduce the guilt? There is not a right or wrong response. It just depends on how the nuance of the language lands for you.

A gratitude practice is also where you might find your ego showing up and telling you that you shouldn't want to grow. It might sound something like, "You are so lucky to have what you do have that you shouldn't want for more. Are you not happy? Do you not love your life enough? Who are you to think this? Just be grateful for what you have. Look at all of those people who are worse off than you!" And so that guilt sneaks in there under the influence of trying to process gratitude. The word *appreciation* lightens that load of guilt a bit (or at least it does for me).

Gratitude, thankfulness, and *appreciation* are so close in meaning that they are used interchangeably, and I will continue to use *gratitude* for our discussion here. But I think this distinction brings a powerful awareness to have and to use as a part of your gratitude practice. You do have the power to call it an appreciation practice if that allows you to release any underlying "should" feelings. If that resonates, I would highly recommend doing that!

Since that guilt sliding in is a common challenge for many (myself included), let's quickly address that topic. Gratitude and goal setting, or gratitude and growth, are not mutually exclusive states. Your dreams and desires are in your heart for a reason and are part of your truth. There is nothing wrong with valuable goals and wanting more on your journey of life. Listening to your heart's desires is an important step to showing up as the way that you really want to show up. It's the path to tapping into your inner light. As you become more aware and compassionate, you can grow and do more good in the world. And that is really what we are all here for! The gratitude for what we have now and where we are now allows us to be able to create that growth from a heart-centered place. It's the most fulfilling way to do it.

Gratitude and sadness can coexist too. Think of my story about being sad and feeling alone after moving across the country. The sweet angel messenger didn't remove the sadness of all of the losses from the move. But it did open up a window to allow for more light to come in, to see the beauty in the present moment. The goal of a gratitude practice is not to negate the challenges but to see the coexistence of the light and the dark and to help us choose to allow more light in.

PART ONE

Why We Build a Gratitude Practice

A gratitude practice is the foundation of intentional living. Just like working out and building muscular strength and flexibility, when you intentionally set a daily or regular gratitude practice, that truly increases your resiliency and your ability to handle stress. We have to work on expanding our ability to feel good. Our bodies are used to being in a state of stress, so we have to offset that with activities that provide better energy. There are extensive studies on gratitude, and some studies even show that people who have a regular gratitude practice are measurably happier than the rest of the population! *(REFERENCE 4: Various Studies on Gratitude Practices and Potential Benefits)* That is an incredibly powerful motivator, especially when we are dealing with so much chaos in our larger world and often in our personal lives as well. Any practice that can create that kind of return on investment seems well worth making a part of your daily life.

Gratitude is the foundation of truly being content. Gratitude gives us a perspective that allows for both grounding and growth. Gratitude is how we shift our perspective. It affects our interpretation of our life. Gratitude is the framework for connecting to our soulful vision and designing our lives to be abundant.

How to Build a Gratitude Practice

There are several ways to approach gratitude, and there isn't a right or wrong way to do this. The reason that so many people talk about having a morning gratitude practice is that it sets the tone and your energy for the day. Some people find it more beneficial to incorporate this at the end of the day and to take that moment of giving thanks when they are winding down. You could choose to have a written practice at the beginning of the day and a quicker reflection practice at the end of the day. The only trick is finding the time that works for you and how your days flow. When you really strengthen that gratitude muscle, you will start to incorporate it throughout your day.

I have found that thinking of gratitude in segments of life is helpful, such as in the following examples:

First, be thankful for the things you know you are thankful for externally: your wonderful family, your home, your friends.

Then go internal: find appreciation for your gifts, your strengths. Recognize the really extraordinary parts of you, and give thanks. Recognize the parts of you that you might deem normal or average, and open up to the possibility that others wish they were that way. Give thanks that you are.

Finally, ponder your challenges: what are the gifts on the other side of your challenges? Give thanks for that silver lining. Express gratitude in your heart for all that you have learned from them.

PART ONE

Integration: Gratitude Practice Approaches

Gratitude Integration, Part 1:
The first approach toward starting a gratitude practice is to keep it easy and start with the obvious: list the things you are thankful for. A common recommendation is to incorporate that morning practice and start each day focusing on three things that you are truly grateful for. This is a great place to start, but I invite you to make it even more meaningful by taking it a step further and to think about why you're grateful for it. Follow that with having gratitude for all the people involved in creating this reality for you. As an example, think about the simple and time-honored practice of giving thanks for your food. The initial and wonderful practice is the first step of blessing your dinner and saying grace every night (many of us did this growing up). But you can create more gratitude by pausing and really savoring the food and savoring the process, giving thanks for the many people who were involved in getting that meal in front of you. Or maybe it's getting that wonderful coffee or tea in front of you. Take that extra moment and thank the farmers who grew it, and thank the truck drivers who got it to wherever you bought it from—the grocery store workers or the coffee shop baristas or whoever and whatever it is. Take some time, decide what you really want to focus on to give that extra depth of gratitude, and either write it down in the journal prompt or take the time to reflect on it and put it out in the universe with your thoughts and your energy around it.

Realize that the little things are beautiful and everything really has so much depth to it. Go on a happiness hunt as you go about your day. Find your appreciation in the little things you see all around you: the flowers, the rocks, the animals, the trees, modern conveniences like our cars and phones. My favorite color is blue, so sometimes on a walk, I might choose to notice everything that is blue and give thanks for that, letting it put a smile on my face. There is no right or wrong here. Express gratitude for every little thing that lights you up!

Gratitude Integration, Part 2:
The second approach to a gratitude practice is to take the heart-centered perspective and express deep gratitude for our loved ones. However, I love the idea of taking this further than just thinking, "I'm so grateful for my family and friends." Challenge yourself to go deeper with this. Think of three people who mean so much to you, with whom you could connect. To make it fast and easy, you could send a couple of quick texts saying how much they mean to you and that you're so grateful for their friendship (or family connection). But then, pick one of those people and take it even further. Spend a little more time on that text or outreach and share with them why you are grateful for them. If you have the time, do this for all three. For example, one of the first times I did this practice, I thought of a friend whose parenting advice has truly impacted my parenting in such a beneficial way for my boys and for me. She made me a better parent, so when I texted her, I told her that specifically! I

PART ONE

invite you to do something similar with someone you love. You may realize that you've never expressed to them why you love them so much! Say something to this effect: "I appreciate you so much, and this is why . . . and I realized I've never told you that and just wanted to share." I think that as we all go through life, one of the most important things that we want is to be appreciated, right? We do appreciate others, but in the rush of daily life, we forget to share this appreciation or might even take them for granted. By stopping to share your gratitude, you will create so much joy for both of you.

Gratitude Integration, Part 3:
Random acts of kindness are so fun and easy. The concept of the random act of kindness is so effective and fun because it helps us to take our elevated sense of gratitude and appreciation and turn it into an action. How do you do this? Let others experience your kindness without any expectation of receiving anything in return. Get creative in the ways you go about this. You can start with simple things, such as holding doors for people, saying thank you unexpectedly, giving compliments to strangers, and giving small things like coffee or flowers unexpectedly or even anonymously. I love the practice of silently sending deep gratitude to service people with whom you don't interact, like the garbage collectors and the snowplow drivers. You could leave positive notes in public for strangers. You could hop online and leave a nice review for a small local business or specific service provider. My personal favorite activity that I've seen other people do, and that is on my to-do

list for myself, is to create a flyer with tear-off tabs at the bottom, and write positive messages on the tabs. The flyer encourages the reader to tear one off and pass it on. How fun does that feel in your body just thinking about it?

Gratitude Integration, Part 4:
Moving from a focus on the little things in life, let's now focus on the big things in life: our experiences. Visualize a moment in your life in which you felt true joy. Was it a big event, or an amazing trip? Close your eyes and let your body feel those feelings of joy that you had in that experience. Sit with gratitude and feel that joy for a while, and when you open your eyes back up, know that you can carry that gratitude and joy with you into your day. For me, that includes my wedding day, the birth of my children, and some amazing moments in travel.

Another type of experience to consider in a gratitude practice is the opposite of looking at the joyful moments. Look at your bigger challenges in life. Maybe it was a difficult childhood, an illness, the challenge of the pandemic, or a stressful time in your career or relationships. How have you grown from those challenges? For what lesson and growth in those experiences can you choose to be grateful? Were there people who supported you? Was it your own tenacity and grit and grace that showed up for you? What were the best moments of these growth experiences? While I grew up in a sometimes challenging household, some of my greatest strengths of harmony and optimism were born out of those chapters of my life.

PART ONE

And finally, think of the accomplishments in your life. What are you proud of? Allow yourself to feel appreciation for your own strengths and gifts that helped you create those achievements. Allow yourself to feel gratitude for the other people in your life that helped you get there. These are powerful questions to write about in a journal and really reflect on with a perspective of gratitude. I am putting writing this book on my gratitude list, along with all of the support from the people who helped me accomplish this.

Gratitude Integration, Part 5:
This approach is about focusing back into us. This is about expressing gratitude and appreciation for our own bodies and our own minds. There are some interesting ways to do this. An easy way to think about it is what is your favorite physical activity or exercise. These can be things that you are able to do that bring you joy. Express your gratitude for the ability to do that. You may have a talent that brings you joy, such as music or art or athleticism or cooking or whatever you are good at. Reflect on those talents and express gratitude for it and why. It's powerful to write these down and see what comes up about shy and how those things bring you joy. For instance, I love yoga and have my 200-hour YTT (yoga teacher training) and will soon complete my 300-hour YTT. However, my lack of flexibility is something that I can get in a negative headspace about. But when I focus on my gratitude for being able to do all that I can do, I am allowing it to fill me up.

Move into your personality traits. What are your strengths and characteristics that you're grateful for, that are a part of who you are? Another gratitude concept is to think of specific parts of your body that you have a positive association with and express gratitude for that. Maybe it's our hands, for their talents and hard work. Maybe it's our feet, for the roads they have carried us down. Maybe it's our womb, for birthing children. Maybe it's our kind eyes. Allow yourself to own what you appreciate about your body, and express and feel that gratitude.

We've all either had the personal experience or have seen family and friends go through big health or other physical issues. This serves to remind us that when our health and well-being is challenged, they become the most important thing that matters. When you are in a state of health and well-being, it's so important to feel and express gratitude for that. A lovely way to express gratitude may be through a prayerful reflection or mantra meditation reflection or affirmation, saying, "I offer gratitude for being able to do this activity. I offer gratitude for my health and well-being. I offer gratitude for being able to play the piano, or cook," or fill in the blank. Again, writing it out may add a deeper sense of insight and gratitude.

If you are going through a physical challenge or a health challenge, maybe you could approach the situation with loving-kindness, compassion, and grace towards yourself and your body and the challenge. Then, thank the parts of the body that are working for you and trying to help you heal and get better. (Know also that

PART ONE

the rest of us are sending you healing prayers, so allow yourself to receive those.)

We don't like to spend much time thinking about ourselves from the perspective of honoring our bodies. It's a truly valuable way to finish out the gratitude practices.

Having gratitude as a part of your daily life is an incredibly powerful tool to level up how you handle everything: the happy things, the little things, the big things, and of course, the stressful things that are a part of life. There are countless ways that you can get creative with incorporating a gratitude practice. Create a gratitude practice with your kids or with a family member or a close friend. It's nice to make it fun and be inspired by each other.

If you do have kids, the practice of asking them to share with you what was the best thing that happened today is an effective way to show them and even train them on how to find the good in the world. It trains their brain to repeatedly and continually look for the good. We really should all do this. Everyone at every age can work on training their brains. Another way to expand on this fun activity is to make a gratitude jar or bulletin board and allow it to become a creative part of your daily life and have others involved.

Your attitude and your gratitude directly correlate with your ability to find the calm in the chaos. The more you incorporate a gratitude practice into your life, the better prepared you will be to handle the next round of hard times. You will have built resilience. The better you feel, the more in touch you are with your own inner light and your own inner peace. Gratitude is living from your heart space and letting that loving energy shine brightly.

DESIGNED TO SHINE

Be proactive in creating a gratitude practice.

You are worthy.

Feel the gratitude in your heart for being worthy.

You are designed to shine.

Allow in appreciation for knowing this truth.

Gratitude will help you rediscover the authentic you.

4
The Wisdom of Journaling

I asked myself, "When you see your future self, living in her highest purpose, what does that look like?" I am an author and spiritual thought leader. I lead large groups in beautiful settings through transformative breathwork and meditation journeys. My energy is one of confidence and graceful strength. People feel inner peace and light radiating and bestowed upon them. Everyone, including me, is shining. I am leading and holding space and abundant.

This is one of my personal journal entries that I like to revisit because it reinforces my vision and purpose.

Now, is that something I would ever say to myself or plan out in a strategy session? Is it something that I would talk about over coffee with a friend? No, those visions don't come from your cognitive mind. They come from connecting with your inner wisdom. They come from creativity and intuition. They come from reflection combined with intention. And they are revealed in the process of journaling.

To create change in your external world, you have to go on the internal journey. Journaling, and especially freewriting, which taps into the creative side of the brain, is a superpower of a tool to help you do that.

The answers are always within you.

You just have to take the time to ask.

I know what you might be thinking.

Are you seriously asking me to keep a diary?

Are you giving me another "to-do" item?

I don't have time for this. I have to go do things!

Do you want to skip this section because these are the thoughts in your head?

The resistance to proactive growth may often sound like our inner teenager.

And if you have parented a teen, you know the best way to approach that attitude is with love and patience. And I promise to keep it short!

Here's the thing: journaling is one of the most effective ways to tap into your subconscious and really explore your thoughts, clearing out the clutter and deepening your self-knowledge. It helps create awareness of who you are right now in this stage of life. It creates mindfulness, giving you a chance to pause and reflect in your own words. You will most likely be surprised by what you put on that paper and discover about yourself and your thoughts.

Journaling is also a great way to practice gratitude.

Journaling is a great way to tap into our creative flow.

Journaling can be a stress release and a place to work through issues.

You will be astounded by what you can learn about your subconscious thoughts, your creative ideas, your ability to release stress and forgive, and your incredible inner wisdom. It will all flow out of you. It just requires deciding to be proactive and participate.

If you have resistance to journaling, you are not alone. We are wired to always be moving and doing, so journaling feels like one more thing that would be in the way of what we are in the habit of believing is more productive doing. But that's where the work and the growth live, when we ask ourselves to stretch out of our comfort zone to see what is revealed to us. Intentional living that elevates and transforms you is not comfort-zone living.

What if we thought of it as a proactive choice to explore our personal growth? You have the power to choose your thoughts around this and decide that you want to see if it works for you.

If you are motivated by the scientific proof of the benefits, there are several studies that support the practice of journaling as well. For a list of a few of those studies, check out the References section at the back of this book *(REFERENCE 5: Various Studies on Journaling and Emotional Well-Being)*.

A great practice is to journal after a meditation and breathwork session. If you want to keep it short, try a minute or two of breathwork, a few minutes of meditation, and a few minutes of journaling. Finding ten minutes in your day is always doable. It's just a decision to make it a priority. And realize that you don't have to make it a daily practice or something that you are committing to forever. Try it for this stage of personal exploration and see what is revealed to you. The questions throughout this chapter are great places to start, as well as any of the questions in the Integration Practices listed at the end of each section.

Integration: Journaling

How do you make time for this? Even if you have set the intention to try to start journaling more, how do you actually integrate and implement this into your life?

There is no one right way of doing things. Don't judge yourself if you didn't journal long enough or often enough. There is no rule concerning freewriting or using prompts. Just try it in different ways, and see what works for you. Create openness to the process.

My favorite journal prompt for any topic is that when your brain answers, "I don't know," give yourself some loving self-compassion, and say, "Yes. But what if I did know?"

Here are some ideas for ways you can choose to make it happen:

1. Make a short-term commitment to the action. Just try it on for a bit and see how you feel about it. Buy yourself a new journal if that makes it more fun.

2. Decide to fit it in. What works for you? Can you journal while you have your morning coffee? Would it be better to write while you wait in the pickup line at school, or on the train commute to work? Do you feel more reflective at night? Is there another activity that you want to tie it to, like journaling after meditation? Commit not just to the action but also to making the time.

PART ONE

3. If adding a ritual makes it more appealing, do that! Light a candle or diffuse essential oils, play some music—whatever works! But don't let the ritual become an excuse for not doing it. Let the ritual part be easy.

4. Are you unsure where to start and feel resistance to free-writing? Use any of the thousands of free journal prompts online to make it easier to start. Use the journal prompts throughout this book. Journal prompts are a fantastic tool to start the flow of writing.

5. Set yourself up for success by putting your journal in a place that you will see it or have easy access to it. Maybe that is on your nightstand, by your morning coffee, or in your purse if you are going to fit it in on the go. If you really want to put it away, it may be helpful to set a reminder to journal. This is how you make it easy for yourself, instead of making it another thing that you wanted to do but forgot about. Keep it front and center.

Change your perspective and commit to a routine, because you want to grow and feel more connected, grounded, and aligned. It can be easy. You can fit it in. You just decide.

PART 1 SUMMARY:

Living Intentionally, Grounded and Embodied in Loving-Kindness

Mantra: I honor and nourish my body by grounding and inviting in loving-kindness to both my inner and outer worlds.

My intention for you in this first section is for you to become more embodied and to be more present in your everyday life, and to nourish and honor yourself through the temple of your body. These practices are, of course, in addition to the movement and nutrition world that we all know is another foundation of living with vitality. The key is that you want to focus on who you are being as you go about each day, not just on what you have to do.

You can use the awareness of grounding practices to drop into the present moment, even if it is as simple as mindfully enjoying your cup of tea. You may decide to incorporate breathwork and meditation to build your mental and emotional resilience, and feel how that strengthens your ability to be present. Over time, you might feel the benefits of stress reduction and choosing new reactions to things. You might finally choose to incorporate that daily gratitude practice and possibly feel your happiness levels growing. You can choose to be astounded at the flow of inner wisdom that may come out of you if you decide to be intentional about journaling. Pulling these all together gives you an incredible toolbox of loving-kindness toward yourself and the world.

PART ONE

These practices may allow in radical self-love and self-care, combining the physical with spiritual and emotional well-being. In my personal life, I have supported myself with exploring additional modalities, like massages, acupuncture, tapping, Reiki, and more. I'm so grateful that there are so many healers in our world, and I highly recommend you use those if they are in your means and interests. But I wanted this section only to include those foundational pieces that are in your control right now, today. This is your commitment to your evolution, your growth, your elevation in the present moment.

Your body and your subconscious mind are operating on autopilot in most areas of our lives, having us repeat habits and patterns, many of which are not serving us. So we have to intentionally reset them. I hope you use some or all of the practices in this section to nurture the sanctuary of your body and live from that elevated state.

From that state, let's explore the concept of more mindset tools and being centered in harmony, another pillar in our journey to true empowerment.

PART TWO

Centered in Harmony—the Empowerment

DESIGNED TO SHINE

Bridge the Gap: A Poem

That space in between—
We had something that we wanted.
We knew it was great.
We loved how great it was.
And then, things changed.

We think of our future,
That beautiful place of possibilities.
We know it will be great.
We love how great it looks to be.
But we downplay the ideas, our place.
And then, things stay the same.

We forget to look around and see the beauty of the now.
We forget that our current life is already great,
Even if it's different than we expected.
There is still so much to be thankful for.
Awareness of the greatness now
Creates the space for that beautiful future.
And then, things start to shift.

We start to be more curious.
We start to see more potential.
We start to feel more self-belief.
We start to move with intentional action—
Just baby steps at first, then strides.
And then, we start to bridge the gap.

PART TWO

We bring the greatness of the future
And the greatness of the past
And the greatness of the present
And combine them into our current state of great.

And then, we have something that we wanted.
And then, we embody our beautiful place of possibilities.
And then, we exude appreciation for the present.
And then, we embrace our potential.
And then, we fill that space in between.
And then, we bridge the gap.

5
Being Mindful of Your Mindset

Are you afraid that you might be bad at something?

What if you are amazing at it?

And what's the worst thing that will happen if you are bad at it?

Are you afraid that the feeling of being overwhelmed and the chaos will never stop?

Are you choosing to sit in a role that no longer serves you?

What's the story that you are telling yourself that is holding you back from really doing what you want to do? Or the story about what is going on in the world around you? Who are you being? Who do you want to be? What could your inner coach tell you about this?

The first time I was introduced to this proactive mindset work to reframe your thoughts was with a wonderful coach. She asked me to identify what the thought was that was holding me back (what was my fear), and then what new thought could replace the old one that would help me create the results I wanted (what was an empowering idea that could replace the fear). This blew my mind at the time. It was so enlightening.

Mindset work is about reframing your thoughts to create these new feelings and actions. This powerful concept creates an internal dialogue with yourself to intentionally choose to reframe your thoughts. This is the work: deciding to override our habitual thoughts with more empowering thoughts. This new thought

PART TWO

pathway is often opened by using loving-kindness toward ourselves.

Life is always throwing us curveballs. We see it on the news in the big tragedies, from a pandemic to natural disasters to humanitarian crises to racism to war. We see it in our daily lives, from the big moments like grief and the small moments like plans getting canceled due to sick kids. The curveballs keep coming, and yet we choose to keep striking out when we don't adjust our swing. (Yes, my boys were baseball players.) That's the mindset game to master—realizing that you can always adjust your swing.

When we react without pausing first, we allow the chaos to consume us and our thoughts, creating feelings that we actually are choosing to allow in, even if we don't realize that the thought was a choice. And those feelings often result in actions that are not representative of how we want to show up. Since this is a recurring habit for most of us, let's look at why we want to change that.

If we look at our personal history and the history of the world, we know that chaos is a part of our human existence. It's not going to stop being a part of our existence. Don't we want to create a more empowering way of being? We want to put ourselves in a position in which we can choose to call on our inner coach in times of chaos, and pause. With practice, you can get in the habit of stopping and asking yourself: Who do I want to be in this moment? How do I want to show up? What do I want to bring to the table? Why do I want to be that way? Realizing that we can take a moment, choose to reframe the situation to approach it from a place of loving-kindness and empowerment, and then create the thoughts and feelings that we want to have around it, is one of the greatest skills we can give to ourselves. This is being mindful of our mindset, and it gets us in a state of being that is more aligned with the authentic version of ourselves.

What is the meaning of and difference in the words *mindfulness* and *mindset*?

While *mindset* is the perspective, *mindfulness* is a practice of accepting how things are in the present, with loving-kindness, to create more happiness in the now.

Combining the two parts of mindfulness and mindset work looks like slowing down and creating awareness about what thoughts are creating our feelings and perceptions, and then exploring what would be an effective new thought that would help us create a different feeling, an improved perception, and possibly a new outcome. It is being mindful of our thoughts, mindful of our mindset. It's approaching all of it with more loving-kindness and less judgment toward ourselves.

After enrolling in a life-coaching certification program myself, I was again exposed to and trained in this powerful mindset practice. Since then, I have witnessed other amazing coaches use these tools with other people and groups. My point in sharing all of the places that I have been exposed to this concept is that the coaching world universally agrees with how powerful this intentional mindset and thought work can be. It's an incredibly effective tool. The exciting part is that you can coach yourself to new ways of thinking with

PART TWO

this practice. We can be mindful of the thoughts we are in the habit of having, and intentionally—proactively—choose new ones. It is a wonderful application to your daily life, and is especially effective in the form of journaling.

I went through a stage of having a pretty significant fear of flying. It had a solid grip on me for a few years. As I became more involved in this personal growth journey of mine, I realized that I could reframe my thoughts around it. I would acknowledge the fear as it showed up, release my self-judgment, thank the fear for its purpose, and then mentally run through a few empowering practices. I would remind myself that pilots and flight attendants do this for a living and wouldn't do it if it was life-threatening, and then I would remind myself of the reason for my travel and the priority of that. I would use a variety of mentally supportive practices, such as prayer and deep breathing. I am now able to read a book on a turbulent flight with much less fear! This reframe of thoughts and mindset support has since served me in a variety of ways and circumstances. I used it during the mental overload of the pandemic. I use it to overcome imposter syndrome. I use it when I need to level up how I show up for a work-related event. I use it when I am frustrated. I use it for personal interactions that might drain my energy. Truly, the applications are infinite, and each time I use it, I am able to create the thoughts and feelings that are more in alignment with the true me.

Thought reframing takes practice. Sometimes we may approach it because we want to reduce a feeling, like my fear of flying. But it's actually the thought behind the feeling that needs to be reframed. The feeling of fear is not actually the fear of flying; it is the fear of dying. So I replaced it with thoughts that supported the reasoning that I was actually in a safe activity. You have to do a little mental digging. For example, if it's fear that is kicking in first, look at it and give it that name. It could sound something like this: "Oh, this is fear. I am familiar with fear and accept that it's normal to feel that way. There's nothing wrong with feeling fear, because my brain is just trying to keep me safe. But this much fear isn't required or relevant. What is a way that I can create more safety right now? What thoughts support me in realizing that the fear is bigger than it needs to be? Is the fear a probable scenario?" Then I will take an action that will bring me a little closer to inner peace. (Sidenote: Of course, this is not advice for when you are in actual physical danger! If you are in physical danger, please seek help or get yourself to safety.)

Intentionally reframing your thoughts, or being mindful of your mindset, will come into play throughout this book. It is one of the best proactive skills to use on your personal growth journey. Every time you question your old stories, you are opening up possibilities to new perspectives and new feelings and new actions.

Integration: Reframing Your Mindset

Use your curiosity toward any area of your life that you'd like to enhance.

PART TWO

Become more aware of your current thoughts, feelings, and actions.

Ask yourself a variety of questions:

- What is the story that I tell myself here?
- Who am I being?
- Is it empowering?
- Is it true?
- Who would I like to be in this story?
- How would I like to act and feel?
- How can I create that?
- Do I have fears?
- How can I show loving-kindness toward myself and my fears?
- How can I embrace a more powerful mindset?

Let your own inner wisdom and inner coach guide your questions. You can talk this out in your head or, even more powerfully, write it out in a journal.

An interesting and possibly fun method to tap into more subconscious thought patterns is to use your less dominant hand to write out the answers to the questions. Or use different color pens for the questions and answers.

This is a great practice to revisit for a variety of life scenarios.

Intentional living to rediscover your inner light is a personal growth path that requires a calm determination to commit to the process and trust the growth and openness. Mindset work, in the form of thought reframing and reflection practices, requires consistency and commitment. Think of it as mindset fitness. You don't work out once or twice and expect to see results. You also don't go from not working out to running a marathon. Approach this mindset fitness like physical fitness. Physical health and strength come from commitment to and work on the temple of your body. It requires sweat and planning and discipline. And the commitment to this is always in the moment. Similarly, nutrition requires planning, commitment, and a positive attitude. You have to make small shifts that will allow for gradual expansion. With time and consistency, you will realize one day that you have created substantial changes. And you will be living from more of a heart-centered place, more in alignment, more radiantly, more purposefully.

Let's move forward with seeing how intentional thought reframing can play a part in rediscovering the authentic version of you.

6
Rediscover the Authentic You

"What do you want?"

Does this question annoy you? Does your brain say, "I have no idea. I am just trying to make it through my to-do list each day."

I totally understand this, and I used to have this response too. It is easy to be caught up in the overwhelming moments. The days go by, and we check all the boxes, except that box of really being connected to ourselves and what we actually want.

There was a moment where my disconnect from my own desires was brought to light for me in an unexpected and even simple way. After I had moved to the Chicago area with my husband and kids, I was in my late thirties and meeting a dear friend from Texas for some much-needed time on a girls' weekend to reconnect with old friends. I was the first of our group arriving to meet my friend, who was already at her family's vacation home. And in this dreamy and fulfilling scenario, I literally couldn't answer what should have been the simple question of choosing between these amazing possibilities that she presented to me: What did I want to do next? Did I want to go have margaritas and watch the sunset? Did I want to grab pizza and sit on the patio? Did I want to go to a fabulous local seafood restaurant? I was at such a people-pleasing stage of my life that I really believed that I only wanted to do what she wanted to do. But she wasn't taking that as an answer: "No, I'm here often enough and can do any of this whenever I want. What do you want?"

This honestly stumped me. I had no idea. No one had asked me that in so long. This is actually so normal at this stage of life: being busy raising a family, juggling career and community commitments, and getting through your to-do list each day. We typically don't have the advantage of ease and time at that stage of life to be asking our loved ones what they want. But what shocked me about that moment was how disconnected I was from my wants, combined with a realization of my people-pleasing habits running the show. I honestly couldn't believe that I couldn't answer. It stuck out to me because I was choosing to believe in my core that I wouldn't be happy doing one of these fantastic options if it was making her uncomfortable in any way. What I really wanted in the moment was for her to decide, because then I would know that we were doing something she wanted, and that would give me some sense of people-pleasing peace. (Exhausting!) Her decision would have eradicated the possibility that doing what I wanted would potentially cause her any discomfort. And truly, in that moment, that's what would have made me happy.

But she forced the subject, and I had to choose. (She's such a good friend!) And we had amazing margaritas at the beach bar and watched the gorgeous sunset. It was my perfect way to start a vacation, and I was completely happy. And I was grateful that she has pushed back and made me make a choice. While the scenery and company was perfect, what stuck with me was the fact that

PART TWO

I was floored at how difficult it was for me to answer. I was also struck by my fear of my answer being the "wrong" one.

Now, I am aware that this example has privilege written all over it, but I feel strongly that this story can resonate across possible scenarios. It isn't actually about where I was or what I was doing. It is about the fact that I couldn't answer the question. The walls I had built up internally were so high that I was disconnected from finding a simple answer to what I wanted. The lack of a practice of self-awareness and reflection, combined with a safe habit of people-pleasing, had put me in a state of actions and decision-making that were muddled from my true internal compass.

We have this societal notion (and people-pleasing notion) that it is loving to put ourselves last. Of course, it is loving to take care of our kids and partners and parents and community and clients, and that is where we find deep fulfillment. But the idea of prioritizing our wants and needs first, or even finding the time for that, is often deemed to be self-centered. Filling our cup before we have filled everyone else's cup is not the typical mode of operation. There can be a lot of judgment, including self-judgment, that surrounds this topic.

Pause here and ask yourself this eye-opening question: Do you know everyone else's favorite ice cream flavor, but you can't remember your own? Maybe you know everyone else's favorite meals or restaurants or songs or activities, but you haven't given much thought to your own favorites in a long time. And it's disheartening to realize you have lost touch with yourself along the way a little bit—or maybe a lot. The challenge is happening because you are pulled in a million directions, wearing all the different hats, and it starts to weigh on you. Maybe you have been recognizing that you have an ache inside, but you aren't able to label why it's there since you are actually generally happy with your life. This is where I was: happy with my family life, happy with my general life, and yet I knew there was a yearning for something, although I had yet to put my finger on it.

So many of us are caught up in our roles that we don't even know who we are outside of all of those roles. We feel disconnected from ourselves. Sometimes it feels like you slightly lost touch with who you actually are, and sometimes it feels heavy and big. It is often caused by the fact that we find ourselves in that place where you have taken care of everyone else for so long that you can anticipate what others are going to want without even considering or remembering what you want for yourself.

That disconnect starts to create feelings of discomfort, feelings of resentment, feelings of wanting more—but more of what?

It's more of being connected to the authentic you. It's more of living in alignment with the authentic you. It's more of reconnecting with yourself and figuring out what you want.

That disconnection of living in multiple roles, defined by our families, defined by what we thought we should do with our lives, defined by our career choice, is often how we lose the ability to know what is authentic for us. Very slowly, over time, we strive for success by living up to everyone else's expectations of us and striving to be good at all the different things. And while the hard work pays off and we do more of it because we find success that way, we can still feel empty. That is because being in alignment isn't about being in your head and being driven by your mind to that success point. Being in alignment is about listening to your heart and soul. The fulfillment will come with rediscovering your heart's desires, and then you can use those skills of hard work and persistence that are driven from the mind to integrate into alignment. This is the growth. This is the ongoing life work that we must do to truly come alive.

We all know stories about the outwardly successful people who are actually still unhappy. They are so busy creating the life that they thought they wanted that they missed out on the everyday beauty of life. And even with great success, they still feel empty and lonely, wanting something more, even when they don't know what that is. If this is you, know that you can turn this around.

Integration: Rediscovering Your Authentic Self

One way that you can practice being in alignment with who you really are starts with becoming more aware of your feelings. Start to pay attention and, as we discussed in the mindset section, you can ask yourself a series of questions: Do you feel good in this moment? Your feelings are great indicators of whether or not you are in alignment with your values. How are you acting and being in this moment? Can you approach it differently to create a better feeling? Is there a more empowering thought that would lead you to this better feeling? Can you ask yourself what you need to shift to make things more aligned with that feeling?

The answers are all inside of you. They really are, but you have to seek them out. You have to be proactive. They might be hidden, deep under layers of stories, and you have to intentionally decide to do the work to find the answers. You have to decide to choose you.

One of the most challenging parts of a personal growth journey is tapping into our power to find our own best insights. They are there. We just have to slow down and ask ourselves and listen. And that probably requires knocking down some walls and peeling away some layers. It definitely requires a lot of loving-kindness.

- What do I want?
- What do I need?
- What would make me feel more alive? More joyful? More appreciative?
- What would make me feel more like me?
- How can I support myself to add more of this to my life today? This week? This month?

Like my story above, I know it is really hard to answer these questions at first.

The best trick to overcoming that is to keep asking the question.

When your brain says, "I have no idea what I want or need," talk back and say, "Okay, I know you don't know right now. That's okay. But what if you did know?" Keep asking. Go deeper. And see what answers come forth.

7
Awaken Your Strengths and Values

In order to rediscover your light, you have to be tapping into your strengths and living in alignment with your values.

In order to light up your world around you, you have to be in touch with the most authentic version of you.

- But what does that mean?
- How do you really know your strengths?
- How can you define your values?
- How do you know if you are in alignment?
- What is the authentic version of you?
- How can you even know the answer to these questions?

It starts with creating awareness. There are amazing tools available for you to go down a path of self-discovery and create that awareness. I always recommend starting with a strengths test and a personality profile, but there are several paths to go down. You may have done one or two of these a long time ago, but it's so insightful to revisit them and learn more about yourself. Additionally, while personality profiles typically stay very similar throughout our lives, strengths and values can definitely be redefined over time.

I have been a lifelong student of myself. My curiosity about how the mind works started before I was ten years old. I remember checking out a book from the library about how to develop what was referred to at the time as "ESP," or extrasensory perception. This can be a sixth sense or even mind reading. This concept was fascinating to me, because we could learn how to use our minds in an expanded way. I remember sitting on my swing set trying to strengthen these skills. After my first big heartbreak, I moved away from the intrigue of the special powers and took a more typical teenage approach and really wanted to understand why and how I could feel so bad, and how I was going to move through it. My upbringing included a lot of religion and Catholic schooling, and the wider scope of the similarity of religions and the even bigger topic of universal spirituality has always intrigued me.

The personal development, self-help, and spirituality sections of the bookstore were my favorite places to browse. This was simultaneously an area of shame for me, as I never wanted to get caught in those areas. I thought that people would judge me for looking at self-help books, or that they would think, "What is wrong with her that she needs to fix? Why does she need self-help?" I always played out the scene in my mind that if I had the misfortune of potentially seeing someone I knew in the bookstore, I would definitely act like I wasn't really looking at these "shameful" personal growth books. The judgment and shame of not already being great and/or wanting more would be too embarrassing to endure if anyone actually saw me there. It was that very loud inner critic and inner ego that was

PART TWO

always trying to get me out of there, and yet it was my inner sage, curiosity, and nudge from my soul that would always take me back.

My fascination with personal growth and the study of ourselves is really an ongoing passion for me. I have happily taken as many of the personality profile tests, strengths tests, and assessments as I can find. I have my clients use them to become more familiar with themselves as well. If it interests you to dig deeper in that area, a quick online search will show you a variety of assessments that are free. These are incredible tools to really understand how you are wired and how to use those insights to enhance the way you approach your life.

According to the Gallup/Clifton StrengthsFinder harmony is my top strength. When I took this test several years ago and discovered that harmony was the top strength for me, I was embarrassed and annoyed to receive this result. That just sounded like a doormat personality to me. And I know much of society interprets it that way, so don't worry if you thought that too. On the DISC profile assessment, Tony Robbins's version of this test puts me in the Harmonizer category. People often describe that as a weakness, as something to let go of, saying that it can be categorized as a limiting belief. But time has given me the gift of realization that this strength is something I am incredibly proud of, and I cannot think of a way of being that the world needs more. Yes, I'll be the Harmonizer. After much reflection, I have come around and see how it is one of my greatest gifts. I'll share more on that a little later.

According to the Enneagram personality profile test, I am an Enneagram 9 (with a wing 1, for those of you that love the Enneagrams). Nine is the Peacekeeper. This is also generally a shunned term by our society; a peacekeeper is seen as a doormat, someone who is passive-aggressive, or who doesn't speak her truth. I am saying these things because I have thought them. But that is the damaged ego speaking as well as society's hustling, "go-big-or-go-home" culture. When I listen to my inner wisdom, I know it's not true that this is a weakness. I love this part of me. It's such a gift to bring the energy of peace to people. Of understanding. Of calm in the chaos. Now I like to think that being a peacekeeper might be what the world needs most.

I did the Kolbe assessment and was blown away at truly understanding how my brain is wired. I did the Human Design assessment and was fascinated by how my birth chart information could be interpreted to reveal so much more about me. As a perpetual student of myself, I absolutely love exploring and utilizing these tools.

This is how I have uncovered and connected an understanding of how I am wired to what are my lifelong interests, gifts, and strengths. It's also an example of how I took my limiting beliefs and self-sabotage around my characteristics and turned them into empowering traits that I love. I stepped into how they are authentically me.

If you are not interested in those tests, or if you just want another tool to learn some insights about yourself, a great exercise is to ask three to five people who you are close to about what they perceive your strengths to be. This may feel vulnerable, but it is also so rewarding to receive nice words about yourself from those close to you. Choose from a variety of people in your life, not just all family or all friends.

For another strength reflection exercise, you can do some self-reflection about when you have been "in the flow" and lost track of time, just doing great work and feeling proud of your tenacity. You were using your strengths in that moment, and it is worth recognizing and appreciating that in yourself.

What would this look like for you? What are your gifts that you have been hesitant to admit that you love? What have you seen in yourself as a weakness that could be a true strength? How can you reframe the thoughts that hold you back from truly being you?

Up to this point, we have discussed the layers of rediscovering the authentic you that include interests, gifts, and strengths. Now let's explore defining your values.

Defining Your Values

Have you ever wanted to really embrace life balance, and yet you keep taking on more projects at work or taking on more clients than you have time to handle? Do you say that you value family more than anything, but then you overschedule your life and the lives of your kids so that you have very little time together? Do you hold travel and adventure as a value, but you make excuses about why you can't go once again? Do you value health and wellness, but you habitually grab junk food? Do you say you value spirituality, but you don't do anything to nourish that part of your life? These are all examples of feeling disconnected from ourselves because our actions are not in alignment with our values.

How powerful would it be to have each of those values as clearly defined pillars of how we want to live our lives? Do you see how much more positively we could make those decisions and take action? Do you see how we would feel more fulfilled if we did?

Defining your personal values is a powerful exercise, as values are the guiding lights for how we want to live our life. They are the driving force and motivation behind our actions. They are ingrained in us, even though we are often not consciously aware of them and how we are shaping our actions around them. Our values can reflect to us who we really are, and they are unique to us. They also change over the course of our life, based on the stage we are in and what is currently important to us.

The benefit of discovering exactly what our values are is that it makes decision-making so much easier and goal-setting so much more aligned. When we identify our values, they will serve as our pillars. When we are living in alignment with our values, we are fulfilled and satisfied. And of course, when we are taking actions or operating out of habit that are not in alignment with our values, that is where we feel internal conflict and disconnection.

The value of family is a great example of how to make new decisions if this feels like a disconnection. It can guide your decisions

PART TWO

regarding your working hours and even your activities. Clients have given me feedback about how valuable it has been to have those values defined for them when they are faced with potential activities and projects that will take away from their family time. This is the power of intention. Many people will say it's what they want, but then the disconnect occurs because they don't intentionally prioritize it.

There are many ways to identify your values. When I work with my coaching clients on this, I remind them that values are typically not an end-goal, as they are more of a way of being. Values are lived—such as joy, compassion, service, or adventure. Consider a couple of substantial questions that will start to reveal your values to you: "What do you want your life to be about? What do you stand for?" Another great exercise is to list a few people who you admire, and list the traits about them that you admire. This will reveal to you your own values by what you see as the beauty of them.

There are examples of extensive value lists generally available that you can browse through for ideas, or you can do some journaling reflection for what comes to you as important life values. As I mentioned above, a list of values may include a variety of core pillars of how you want to be living and what you want to be prioritizing in your life, such as beauty, adventure, ambition, respect, status, or freedom. One trick of narrowing down to define your core values is that you want to be really honest with yourself and not listen to the "should" prompts coming from your brain. Your brain might tell you that you should value independence and that you should not value recognition, but if in your heart the opposite is ringing true, listen to that and follow that lead. What resonates as your truth is your truth.

The next step is to narrow down the list to a smaller number of your core values, which can become the pillars for your decision-making around the design of your life. There isn't a magic number, but generally getting your core values down to five or less is the most useful. One way to do this is to rank each of the values you have come up with. Think about the feelings they create in your body, and let yourself become aware of how much you want that in your life. Consider the top-ranked ones as your potential core values.

When you have identified them, you can explore how to experience more of that value in your life. For example, if creativity is a value for you, you can intentionally decide to add more creativity in your life in any multitude of ways.

This is how to rediscover and connect with the authentic you. It is such a significant way to use your inner compass to create a daily life that is in alignment with who you are at your core. A life that is in alignment with your values will allow you to be in a state of inner peace. It will allow you to shine your light.

I went through a career stage that I loved as a passion project but that wasn't actually aligned with the stage of my life. When I was in my forties, one beautiful Chicago summer night we were socializing in my friend's backyard. It was a gathering of a few dozen women, many of whom I didn't know well. And one woman was

PART TWO

telling the story about her interest in attending professional makeup school. A recurring story that I told myself repeatedly in my life was that my actual dream job was to be a makeup artist. This information about a local school stopped me in my tracks, as I had assumed (without having any actual information or research behind my assumption) that makeup artistry schools would only be in New York City or Los Angeles. Could I do this as a middle-aged adult? Could I go to a professional makeup artistry school and finally, officially, learn how to do this? I knew when the words were spoken that I had to research it, and I had to do it if it was good—which I did. Yes, I was in a class with eighteen- to twenty-eight-year-olds, and it was amazing and creative and humbling and exciting and so much fun. After a lifetime of wondering if I could actually do it, I finally answered that calling. It was a layered choice of aligning with some of my values (but not with others, which is why I let it go). Beauty was a value of mine (which really has a deeper meaning to me than external beauty), so I stepped into knowing that it felt right. While that career is not what I am currently doing, it was a major stepping stone to deciding to inspire women to step into the most empowered version of themselves. The experience was an impactful part of my story. It was a part of my journey of tapping into the authentic version of me, aligning with my values and passions. It brought me joy and expanded my world and vision. (It also showed me the importance of aligning decisions fully with all of your pillars, as family time is a primary value of mine with teen boys, and that career directly takes away from family time with teens.)

DESIGNED TO SHINE

Nutrition and a healthy lifestyle have also been an interest and strong value of mine for over twenty years. If I was not proactive about my health issues, I would most likely be dealing with a more significant autoimmune issue. I started questioning what was going on with me in my early thirties and dove deep into research around the issues happening and the impact nutrition had on it. I empowered myself with knowledge, made a lot of changes, and shared this information with those whom I love. But did that mean it was a part of my purpose and calling? Even though health was a strong value of mine, should I combine it with my strengths and start a business around that? This was an easy "no" for me. I knew it wasn't my passion and therefore not my path, even though I felt more empowered and knowledgeable on the subject. I did a good gut check and just knew it was not in alignment for me to pursue that. It didn't speak to me as the soulful vision of my life. And yet, let me say that I am grateful that it is a passion for many people, as I have learned so much from them. When those nutritionists and health coaches stand in their passion, strengths, and values, they are fulfilling their soulful mission and improving the lives of others, like me. That is the beauty of the uniqueness of all of us. Shine your light, my friends. We all need what you have to share.

When you are in alignment, your ability to shine your light just happens naturally. Your ability to tap into your calm persistence, your centered determination, just comes easily. Alignment gives you the ability to drop into your heart's guidance, to find your calm in the chaos, and to be the light in the room.

PART TWO

You are worthy of being in alignment with the authentic you.
You are worthy of the inner peace that alignment brings.
Your heart-centered alignment is a gift to the world.
You are designed to shine.

Integration: Strengths and Values

Mindset practice: We can shift our perspectives by shifting our thoughts. We can create more productive feelings and emotions by shifting our perspectives. One of the most effective ways to shift that perspective and train our brain to think new thoughts is to really look at the current feeling and ask yourself why you feel that. Create awareness about the thought behind it. And then ask, "Is that really true? Is it 100 percent true?" Because whatever is going on around us, in most scenarios, it probably isn't 100 percent true. And with that awareness, you can then ask yourself, "What would be a more empowering thought? What would be a more empowering feeling? What would be a more empowering action from this new thought and feeling?"

Authenticity Journaling Practice
- What truly lights me up?
- When I am at my best and feeling so good, what am I doing?
- What would make me feel like the truest version of me that I've ever been?

Strengths and Values Practice

Work through the questions in the sections above, including the following:

- What are your greatest strengths?
- What are you good at?
- What do you enjoy doing?
- What do you want your life to be about?
- What do you stand for?
- Where do you feel like you are really living into your values?
- What values feel important to you that are missing from your life?
- And yet, let me say that I am grateful that it is a passion for many people, as I have learned so much from them.
- Who do I admire and what values do they have that feel important to me?

There are also a variety of value idea lists online. Write out several values that feel important to you, and work through the process above to create your short list. If you start with a list of forty or fifty values, try to pick a top-ten list, and then narrow it down to a list of the top-three or top-five. These values can be used as your guiding lights for how you make decisions about your actions and activities.

8

Be the Peacekeeper of Your Heart and Soul

What if being the peacekeeper of your heart and soul was actually the most important role you could step into?

Why are we so disconnected from the feeling of ease within ourselves? And why do we have resistance to it?

I worked in corporate banking for almost a decade with great financial success and with great people. But there were many long hours and travel that you think would be glamorous but was actually exhausting. I worked as a stay-at-home mom and volunteer leader for almost two decades, which is very purposeful but also exhausting, with the endless tasks, emails, and to-do lists. Whether it's the corporate or entrepreneurial hustle culture or the hamster wheel of parenting and working and volunteering and doing a million things at once, we are often left feeling depleted. We are running from one part of our lives to the next, never fully present in one place, feeling like we just need to get through this one stage, this one project, this one thing—and then, we'll find more success. Then we'll find more happiness. Then we'll take better care of ourselves. Then we'll find the time to create that space to reconnect with the feeling of ease and inner peace. Then we'll be worthy of it. Then we will be enough.

But what if the answer is that we are worthy of it right now?

What if the answer is that we are enough already?

What if the ease and peace is within us, and it's exactly what our soul needs?

Becoming the peacekeeper and caretaker of your soul is the most important part of our journey. We are here to be happy. We are here to love and be loved. We are here to live in ease and grace and flow and beauty. We are worthy of all of that.

But we get tripped up. Life is messy and difficult along with that beauty. We get into routines, sometimes decades in the making, and we lose our way. Our hearts get broken. Let's be honest: getting to this place of ease and grace and flow isn't easy or graceful or smooth. It's a bumpy dirt road that can get pretty uncomfortable along the way.

Also, becoming the peacekeeper of your heart and soul is not about suppressing feelings or toxic positivity. It's actually the opposite. You want to feel your feelings and process them so that they don't subconsciously control you. You want to empower yourself with loving-kindness to see and witness the hard parts, and then gracefully move into the beautiful parts.

Let's revisit the beauty of the concept of being the peacekeeper, specifically in the context of becoming the peacekeeper of your soul. Set aside the ego's chatter for a minute about peacekeepers being a weakness. What the ego is talking about is the version of self-sacrifice and martyrdom when you lose yourself in people-pleasing. Let that concept go for this discussion.

PART TWO

Put your hand on your heart, close your eyes, and ask yourself, "Would I love to be the peacekeeper of my soul?" Does it resonate? Wouldn't it be worth it to prioritize that ability? Would your soul appreciate that? I'm venturing to guess that since you are here reading this book that your answer is yes. Let's explore a few ways that you can strengthen this part of you.

Integration: Peacekeeping through Self-Care

I am the queen of my version of self-care. The typical way people think of self-care is as exercise and a bubble bath, and let's just say that I am not the queen of either of those things (although I strive to have more of both in my future!). While I do work out, a consistent exercise routine has always been a sticky point for me. And while I am a mostly healthy eater, I have been known to down some Christmas-colored M&M chocolates while ordering a juice cleanse off of the Internet. So why do I call myself the queen of self-care?

My version of self-care is *soul-care*. I am the peacekeeper of my soul. I am the calm in the chaos. And I want to share that perspective with you. I invite you to create that retreat for your soul that will fill you up.

Many people view self-care as another item on their to-do list, causing eye-rolling and sighing. It might fall to the bottom of the to-do list, and it might even sometimes generate a thought of "I wish—must be nice." We might say it to ourselves because we have heard it said about others, or we may have said it about others.

Realize that this is a reflection of the person saying it actually wishing that they treated themselves this way, that they wish it was a priority in their life. So when we think it for ourselves, that's an opportunity for the practice of being mindful of our mindset. That's a thought that can be reframed. You can make the choice to empower yourself here by choosing a new thought and a new feeling. We cannot show up for others from a true place of generosity and love when we have fully depleted ourselves. Self-care is not selfish. It teaches those around us not only how to treat us but how to treat themselves as well. Your loved ones are mirroring your actions. And they will feel more connected to you when you are more connected to yourself.

Connecting and creating our inner peace is the greatest gift we can give to ourselves as well as to those who love us. Take a moment and place both hands on your heart. Envision yourself as having that connection to your inner peace. How does it feel in your body? How does it feel in your soul?

Can you show yourself enough love that you become the peacekeeper of our soul?

Can you see the connection of nourishing yourself and finding inner peace?

Do you know that your inner peace is up to you? And that you are the only one who can give it to yourself?

Do you know that you can strengthen your capacity to be the calm in the chaos, even when the world is hard? Especially when the world is hard?

PART TWO

When you strengthen your capacity for inner peace, you are literally protecting your body, mind, heart, and soul. Finding inner peace does not mean that challenging times will be avoided. It means that you can face those challenging times with so much more ease, grace, and flow.

This requires deciding to strengthen our skills in this area now, whether we are in a time of chaos or calm in our lives. When we are in times of life that feel a little easier, we might not fit in the self-care habits because we are feeling good enough, so we don't think we need it. And then when things get stressful and chaotic, we often think that we will get around to the self-care that we need when things slow down. Yet we all know that things never truly slow down. We have to make the choice and create the time.

Let's revisit meditation as a self-care practice. There is an old Zen saying that says something like this: "You should sit in meditation for twenty minutes a day. Unless you are too busy, in which case you should sit for an hour."

Don't worry; no one is actually asking you to meditate for an hour. You get to choose how to approach this. Would you start with five minutes? If your brain is telling you that you don't want to sit, you can decide to spend five minutes in silence somewhere, maybe on a walk or run. As we discussed earlier, the reason that we come up with amazing ideas in the shower is typically because it is our place of silence. Can you find ways to give this space to your mind and soul elsewhere in your day?

Meditative practices are not the only form of self-care and soul-care. Looking at self-care as a loving action toward yourself, as an act of kindness, automatically turns it into soul-care. Love is a verb, and self-care is an intentional action. Ask yourself these questions: How can you love yourself more? What do you need? Is it fitness and nutrition? Is it slowing down? What brings you joy? What lights you up? What will nourish your body, mind, and soul? It's all unique to you. The gift of giving yourself a few minutes of silence will help you hear your internal answers to these questions.

Nourishing your body is self-care and soul-care. This may include fitness, movement, nutrition, hydration, and the beautiful body practices that detox, such as a salt bath, a sauna, or a massage. Our body is our human temple of our soul, so taking care of it is life-enhancing for all aspects of our existence. Without our health, the rest of the self-care becomes difficult. So this is the starting place and the foundation.

Nourishing your mind is self-care and soul-care. This may include intellectual stimulation, such as reading or learning new skills or personal growth. It may be following a creative endeavor, such as music or art. Your mind may need a digital detox. Our mind is the driver of our body and existence, so keeping it happy and healthy is also life-enhancing and expands our inner peace.

Nourishing your soul is obviously the ultimate soul-care. It includes the most life-enhancing practices that you can participate in. It is connection, joy, laughter, loving-kindness, and being in nature. Being present and experiencing each moment with love

PART TWO

bring you closer to inner peace. This is what your soul wants and needs.

And finally, to nourish it all—the body, mind, and soul—meditation, breathwork, and journaling are the embodiment tools that I have experienced that can tie it all together. They pull in the body's chemical reactions to meditation and breathwork, which fuel the mind and fulfill the soul. There are other modalities (like tapping and somatic healing techniques) that are also amazing soul-care practices. But breathwork, meditation, and journaling are so accessible that I find them to be the easiest to decide to incorporate into daily life. Yes, you can make a beautiful morning routine out of them. Or you can approach it with messy determination: fitting it into your existing day, and no one has to know you are doing them. You can do them anywhere. Do some gentle breathing at your desk. Type journal notes into your phone. Talk a silent meditative walk outside.

How do I fit in self-care? How can I call myself the queen of such practices? Well, I go through stages. Sometimes I love a good morning routine that includes meditation and journaling. But I know I need flexibility and fluidity in my life. It depends on where I am and who is around. It depends on my day ahead. For the meditation piece of it, I use silence, I use apps, I use music, and I use recordings from teachers who I love. I make it a priority and I find a way. For the body detox, in addition to a decade-plus of green smoothies and healthy lifestyle choices, I am actually the queen of the infrared sauna. It is so good for you! There is so much readily available research. I will just say that you should check it out and go—and as a bonus, you can meditate while you are in there! As I mentioned, my challenge for my self-care is sticking to a consistent workout routine and cutting out more sugar. I do the work to connect to my motivation, to release the resistance, and to balance self-compassion with action and integration.

Another idea that I recently started implementing is planning out the podcasts or other educational videos that I want to listen to or watch. If you make a weekly schedule of what you want to listen to, and actually plan what your intellectual stimulation is for the day, you will be so much better about fitting it in. Listen to them on a walk or while driving, cooking, or getting ready for the day. Just like you do meal planning, you could choose to do some podcast planning or personal lesson planning. I have found it to be so much more effective than just trying to decide on the fly what to listen to.

There are countless ways of adding what you need in your life to fill your cup. It's just that you have to decide and make the choice to fit it into your life. This is how you nourish yourself. You must love yourself first to find inner peace.

Integration: Peacekeeping through Self-Integrity

The follow-through is the hardest part, right? I have definitely felt that way in so many areas of my life: writing this book, sticking to an exercise routine, creating better habits, and so on. There is nothing more important than keeping your promises to yourself. You can do all the goal setting and idea generation that you want

PART TWO

(this is literally one of my favorite activities). But if you don't integrate these ideas, you lose self-integrity. You let yourself down. You lack accountability with your own being. And that flows out into the rest of our life and how we show up. It's an energy that other people feel, whether they know the details or not. It's actually who we are being.

It's so fascinating how much resistance our brain creates to any change that we desire to create. We need to remind ourselves that our brain's job is to keep us safe. We can be aware and thank it for doing its job, and literally talk back to our brain. We can let it know that we are making some changes that will actually be for the good of our whole being.

This is where I believe that using meditation, breathwork, or journaling are the most powerful tools to tap into your self-integrity and your inner coach. These options are free to everyone and have been shown by science that they can help you rewire your brain. Tap into your inner cheerleader to override those existing thought patterns and create new pathways in your brain.

Accountability is an important part of self-integrity. It is also easy to create (even though our brain tries to tell us it's hard). You can create a checklist of what you want to add to your life each day, week, or month. You can add reminders on your phone of positive thoughts or actions you want to take. You can ask a friend or family member to be an accountability buddy with you. Truly, the ideas and options are endless. It's just our thoughts that have to be overcome. Use accountability to your advantage so that you keep your self-integrity intact, which keeps your inner peace intact.

Speaking in front of even small groups was a fear I dealt with for most of my life, and yet that fear was a block to shining my light. I sat in the back in class in high school and didn't raise my hand. I was mortified when I was called on because I hated speaking in front of a group. I remember in college having to give a presentation in front of a pretty small class, and even though everyone else had to give similar presentations, that didn't lessen my fear of being seen and not covering the topic correctly. My whole body was shaking, my voice was shaking, and it was probably a very average presentation. In the corporate world, I remember sitting in a conference room on a call with multiple people, on the phone with even more, and I had a great idea and solution come to mind for the topic at hand. I was just a few years out of school, meaning that I was one of the youngest in the meeting, and I doubted my ability to provide value and insights. I was too scared to share my ideas, scared that if it was a bad idea that I would look like a fool. Someone else eventually brought up a similar solution and was given significant praise. I was so disappointed in myself for not overcoming my fear and showing everyone that I had these great ideas too. This memory has stuck with me all these years because I let the fear of appearing foolish override my gifts and ability to contribute. And that is not living in alignment with the authentic version of me. It literally hurt my soul. It took away my inner peace.

Take that part in: the fear of appearing foolish was larger than my confidence in my value, and therefore, my gifts and ability to contribute were kept in hiding.

PART TWO

This is a recurring pattern I see that so many of us struggle with. Several of my coaching clients have been looking to make career changes or get back into the workforce after taking several years to raise their children. In most of these scenarios, the fear says, "What if I'm not good at this new role?" One of the best ways to check in with yourself is to ask, "But what if I'm great at it?" Does it excite you? Does it resonate with your soul? Does it seem like even if the time commitment might be significant, it could still bring you an overall inner peace?

And what if it doesn't work out? What's the worst that can happen in that situation? You learned and you tried. Isn't that better than not trying at all?

This is one of our greatest lessons and challenges in life: knowing that fear is not going away, and we should take the chance anyway.

As I mentioned earlier in the book, I decided to attend makeup artistry school in my mid-forties. I was older than my classmates by twenty to thirty years. That aspect was fun and entertaining in and of itself. But the bigger message that I was sending, both to these younger classmates and to my peers, was that you can decide to jump into whatever your soul is tugging at you to do at any age. It's never too late, and you are never too old. This was me finally doing something creative that I had wanted to do since I was a child. This was me stepping into my self-integrity. And people all around me were intrigued and happy for me.

Was there fear? Absolutely. It's not easy to step so far out of your comfort zone.

Was there failure? Absolutely. There were a few days (like the mature model day) that I thought I would kill it and impress everyone, and instead I wanted to crawl into bed and hide afterward.

Was it the answer to finding my life purpose? Yes and no, as it isn't the career I am in anymore. But here is the key: it was the path I needed to walk to get to where I am today. It opened up the portal to joy, to something that was just for me and wasn't a part of any of the other roles I had defined in my life. It was me standing in my self-integrity, and that felt so good! And that access to integrity and joy then led me further down my path of purpose.

Interestingly, becoming the peacekeeper of your heart and soul most likely will require you to step into your fear. Often, fear is coming from the fight-or-flight part of our brain, which is keeping us from listening to our heart, our gut instincts, and our inner knowledge. While fear is trying to protect us and keep us safe, it is actually creating more inner disconnection when we don't follow through, when we don't show up as the highest version of ourselves that we know we can be. Becoming the peacekeeper of your soul is the way to overcome that. Balance the fear with courage, balance the chaos with your own inner calm, and balance the head with the heart.

Step into your self-integrity. Society typically calls this gaining peace of mind. I see it as gaining peace of soul. When you reconnect with who you are at your core, you can connect to others so much

PART TWO

more completely. This is letting your light shine. This is the key to finding the calm in the chaos.

This is the key to heart-centered being and soul-centered living.
This is how you live in loving-kindness with yourself.
This is how you live in harmony with yourself.
You are worthy of honoring your self-integrity.
You are designed to be the peacekeeper of your heart and soul.

Integration: Peacekeeping with Boundaries

Have you ever gone bowling as a kid, or taken your kids bowling, and the alleys have those bumpers in the gutters so that you (or your kids) don't lose the ball every time? The ball just keeps rolling, bouncing off the sides sometimes. Wouldn't it be nice to put those up in our life, and keep our energy and soul in the game? We all know that gutter balls aren't any fun for anyone.

Many things can cause our boundaries to be stretched and cause those gutter balls to fall in. This often presents itself as the more challenging relationships in our lives, either with people who we perceive as difficult or with work that has overwhelmed our lives.

But the stealthy version of this issue, the one that is painful to realize, is that we have done a lot of this to ourselves. The boundaries we set are not just with other people, but most importantly with ourselves. And that is the first place we can start to honor ourselves more.

We have allowed our own boundaries to be crossed due to believing that our roles require us to show up in a certain manner. And then we often self-sabotage with bad habits to numb out our feelings of disconnect. Then those boundaries that we have crossed with ourselves are often just distraction techniques and people-pleasing techniques. We often don't realize that we are doing it because it is such a habit and part of how we operate our lives.

Quiet boundaries are often crossed because we live in a state of thinking about what we should do. We need to be careful how we talk to ourselves from a place of "should." Maybe we signed up to volunteer for things that we don't want to do because we thought we should. Or we said yes to a dinner with a difficult relative because we thought we should. Or we took on another work project because we don't want to disappoint our peers, and we want to look capable of taking on more. Or we take on the role of the martyr stay-at-home mom and live an overscheduled life of running our kids around but never prioritize ourselves. We over-caffeinate and under-hydrate. Then we numb ourselves by binge-watching TV shows, eating pizza, and drinking wine, because we worked so many hours that we feel like we deserve it. And then we don't feel good enough to fit in exercise, connect with friends, or eat well. Do you see the vicious circle? Do you see all of the gutter balls just falling in?

And then have you ever followed up that numbing-out cycle with one of too much exercise and strict healthy eating, only to have it fall by the wayside because it was too extreme to live life that way? I have. Gutter ball.

PART TWO

Let's instead approach the boundary setting with self-compassion and loving-kindness. Allow yourself the grace to see that many of these things are just routines you fell into that grew over time. And now you can celebrate yourself, because you are going to start making some of these small shifts to set those boundaries and create more inner peace.

It takes some reflection to figure out what the easy first shifts would be that you could make. It takes a little bit of tough self-love to see where you need to set boundaries for yourself and not try to please other people. Look at where you are being a yes-person, and decide to say no where it makes sense to honor your own needs. By learning to say no, you are also learning to say yes to your soul, which is in fact where your desires and your dreams are waiting for you.

The power of choosing to listen to your inner coach who speaks with the voice of loving-kindness is the key to ultimate inner peace. If you hear a judging inner coach, the voice of "should," that's the wrong voice—that's the inner critic. Taking the time to check in with your inner knowledge and following through on that is so important to inner peace.

Intentionally setting boundaries for ourselves and others is the ultimate in self-care. When you are no longer depleted, you are so much more capable of staying calm in the chaos. Making these changes and implementing more boundaries is best accomplished with small, doable shifts. The extreme shifts usually lead to feeling disappointed in yourself when you fail.

Setting boundaries in personal relationships is a very complicated part of this topic and deserves its own book. Here I am not addressing any relationship that puts your safety into question (and I very much want you to seek assistance with that). I'm also not addressing marital or dating issues. But I understand the challenge of having difficult and even gas-lighting extended family members or social situations. There are often people in our lives who we may not have to deal with every day, but they are a part of our lives. We have to find a better way to interact with them that allows the relationship to still exist and allows you to honor yourself and your needs. One of the boundaries to navigate when working through personal relationships is to figure out when walking away is necessary and when creating space is necessary. But there are circumstances when those aren't options, and we have to find a way to live with the situation. What do we do then?

My favorite technique that I have found helpful when I have to deal with challenging relationships that drain my energy is to use the power of intentional thought reframing. Additionally, you can visualize how you want to show up and how your energy is protected, or you could create mantras and affirmations that provide you energetic support as you approach the situation. The best place to start is preparing your own energy before you begin to interact with these people. Using the voice of your inner coach, you can choose to accept that you can handle the difficult part for the amount of time you are interacting with them, and that you are wearing an invisible blanket or a bubble of energy protection that allows any words or

PART TWO

negative interactions to bounce off of you and fall away. Or maybe you see those gutter-ball guardrails up, and you are the ball that doesn't fall into the negativity and the gutter. You are no longer absorbing the challenges of the interactions, and you are letting them bounce off of you. You can choose to see the good parts of them and energetically send them peace and kindness. These thoughts alone will give you so much more power and peace for the duration of the interaction, and the recovery period afterward will hopefully be so much shorter. I know that this has been the case for me and for some of my clients. This practice takes time and intention, but it is so worth it to become the peacekeeper of your soul.

It's also incredibly important for our inner peace to create boundaries for social media and digital communication as well. Our digital life has created a situation in which boundaries are required. When we start our days with checking email and notifications and social media statuses, we are allowing all of those outside influences to affect us from the moment we wake up. It is taking up mental space right away. While there are many amazing benefits of our electronic communication world, we have to protect our mind and energy by placing boundaries on when we check and use them. When you start your day by checking email and social media accounts, you put yourself in reaction mode, with the stress of the to-do list and comparison with others at full speed. It's really difficult to shine your light with the world from a place of reaction. If instead you chose to start your day with quiet reflection time and set intentions for how you want to feel that day and prioritize what is important to you, you are going to be in so much more control of your energy. You are going to show up for your to-do list with intention, allowing you to approach life with a calm determination instead of a chaotic reaction state. As I mentioned in the introduction to this book, the small steps to shining your light and living in alignment with your soulful vision of your life are only possible through intention, not reaction.

This requires you to commit to a growth process that is not found outside in the world somewhere. It is a growth process that has to happen from within.

Alignment, integration, and mindset are the keys to being the peacekeeper of your soul. The most heart-centered role you can play in this life is to be the proactive peacekeeper of your soul.

You are worthy of cultivating supportive boundaries for yourself.

You are worthy of creating harmony for yourself.

You are enough.

Your inner light is your connection to your soul.

Let it shine.

9
Embracing Harmony and Duality

Definitions of harmony:

1. The combination of simultaneous musical notes in a chord

2. A pleasing arrangement of parts

3. Internal calm, agreement, tranquility

4. An interweaving of different accounts into a single narrative

There is a natural rhythm of harmony. It is in music. It is within you.

I grew up in a household filled with a lot of polar opposites in people and in circumstances.

My dad was six feet, three inches tall.

My mom is five feet, one inch tall.

My dad was a Protestant, raised Baptist, played as the organist in Lutheran churches for forty years.

My mom is a devout Catholic who loved going to daily mass and considered being a nun.

My dad was a Republican.

My mom is a Democrat.

My three siblings and I were born and spent the first part of our childhoods in upstate New York, moved to Alabama for a few years, and then moved to Texas. We were exposed to a wide variety of cultures within those moves.

There was plenty of alcohol.

And plenty of religion.

There was extreme anger and fear.

And there was a lot of love.

There were traumatic moments.

And joyful moments.

There was connection and disconnection.

There was both community and isolation.

There were rule-followers and rule-breakers. (My siblings and I were actually split down the middle on this one; I was on the rule-breaker side for some angst-ridden teenage years.)

There was musical harmony played in our home. (My favorite memories with my dad were when we played piano duets in what I remember as perfect harmony.)

And there was discord over many issues of life.

And from these blessings and these challenges, my greatest strengths and gifts emerged.

I am the observer and the peacekeeper.

I know how to read a room.

I know how to hold space for others.

I see both sides, and I know how to bring harmony to situations so that everyone can rise and come together with grace and compromise to get what they want most (if it serves the greater good).

I see the benefits of differences and what they bring to the table.

I see that there is truth in all of it.

It's a gift to see both sides and want to bring those sides to a greater communion of understanding and coexistence.

While some of these strengths and gifts were caused by my environment, I believe more of it is inherent in how I am wired. My three siblings grew up in the same environment, and it allowed their life experiences to develop their strengths and gifts in very different ways.

Interestingly, my siblings and I are diverse versions of generational pattern-breakers. Many people see the bad part of their upbringing and re-create it anyways. If this is something you realize you are doing, know that you can decide at any time that there is a different way, a better way. You can decide to create more harmony in your life by choosing to be a generational pattern-breaker. That is when you are creating harmony for your higher self.

Harmony is a form of alignment. Harmony is a form of integration. And harmony is a mindset.

Harmony is applicable to everyone's life, both internally and externally. To create harmony within your body, mind, and soul is to create a beautiful place to exist. Our existence is complex, in that our body, mind, and soul make up the oneness of us, and yet they are three separate parts of us to nourish and balance. When we are out of alignment in one area, we feel it everywhere else within us. It's like our own divine trinity within our one being. And we are all just trying to get those three parts of our one being into a state of harmony.

Just like music, the different parts of life can be brought together to make a beautiful harmony. The chorus of life can bring together so many different parts in such a beautiful unison if we choose to see it that way.

It can be a choice to see the harmony of life. You can compose your own new harmony at any time you choose. Your intentional living can be focused on cultivating harmony.

When you are in harmony with the world around you, your inner light and inner peace will naturally come through you. Your ability to tap into your calm in the chaos will be easy when you are coming from a place of harmony. When you tap into your heart as a guide, the world looks a little more grounded in harmony.

In a life filled with chaos and discord, choosing harmony and joy is the courageous choice. It is the heart-centered choice. It is the light-filled choice.

Alignment, integration, and mindset work are the keys to creating harmony in your life.

Harmony will help you to feel grounded.

Harmony will bring inner peace.

PART TWO

Integration: Steps to Connecting with Harmony

There are two parts of sharing my story and my strengths for you to take away and do your own reflection. One is to look at harmony, and the other is to look at your life story.

1. Harmony can be a guiding light in relationships and with yourself. Start to strengthen your curiosity about the other side of situations, about what people might want. Open yourself up to observe and see if more ideas are revealed that could be empowering for all. This is what countries do in peace negotiations. This is what mediators strive to accomplish. And there is power in seeing where we can use that in our daily lives. Do you allow for the harmony to emerge from your life? Where could you let more harmony in? How could your body, mind, and soul be in more harmony?

2. Look for the stories from your childhood that have actually defined some of your greatest strengths. Have you seen them that way before? Do you lean into those strengths? How could you align more closely with your values and strengths? Would you create more harmony in your life if you were living more in alignment with your values?

Another great way to find more harmony in life is to realize that many of the things that we think are mutually exclusive are not. They are not the single chords we think they are, and they are actually so much more beautiful together. The duality of seemingly opposite things is often where the most beautiful harmony is composed.

Integration: Embracing "And": The Gifts of Duality

I remember being at my grandparents' funerals and watching my parents and their loved ones both laugh and cry. That mix of sadness and laughter showed up for my dad's funeral too. It's an interesting place to be, isn't it? A funeral reception is often a place where you can witness and accept the concept of duality. Hopefully, there is laughter and deep love coinciding with flowing tears and sadness. It's a beautiful thing, and interestingly, it's not something we really allow for in many other places.

This gift of duality, of allowing a balance between seemingly opposite things to exist together, actually creates a richer experience. Sometimes allowing that space, in your thoughts and in your life, brings forth a beautiful harmony that you never would have seen otherwise.

We tell ourselves these stories that two things shouldn't coexist together.

When we feel gratitude, we might throw in some shame for wanting something more.

When we feel grief, we might throw in that shame for laughing and feeling joy.

PART TWO

When we feel stressed, we shame ourselves for the anxiety, thinking of all the other people in the world who have it worse and that we shouldn't be feeling what we do.

When we feel our gifts shining through, we feel imposter syndrome and tell ourselves to take it down a notch and that it was luck or that we really don't belong.

When things are chaotic, we might not realize that we can still be calm.

This is the opportunity to become aware and reframe unproductive thoughts.

This is the place we need to come to for self-acceptance and allow ourselves to feel what we are feeling, without shame, without belittling ourselves.

Our difficult emotions need to be felt and to be allowed to exist in order for us to process them.

And we can choose a new thought about the hidden gifts in the pain.

The silver lining is always there. We just have to be open to seeing it.

Consider the possibilities and allow space for things to coexist that you have traditionally thought of as mutually exclusive. Take a good look at your strengths, gifts, and life lessons, and consider how you can use them from a heart-centered place that would light you up.

As the integration exercise, I invite you to journal on these questions:

- Do you have a life story that has been a challenge for you that you could also see as your greatest lesson?
- What if you choose to see the harmony of your strengths and gifts and life lessons and turned them into your superpower?
- What if you listen to your inner knowledge and trust that message?

This is the same wisdom of the ancient Chinese philosophy of yin and yang. These opposites are complementary and are the flow of life. Here's a quick list of seemingly opposite things that are truly so much richer together. See what this list sparks in you to generate your own ideas or stories of opposites that are better together, like the rainbow that is possible because of the rain. It is a bridge of harmony that makes the coexistence of these an improvement from their existence alone.

Light and darkness
Effort and ease
Strong and soft
Messy and beautiful
Boundaries and freedom
Difficult and easy
Preoccupied and present
Fearful and courageous
Patience and urgency
Masculine and feminine

PART TWO

Happiness wouldn't be a great emotion without sadness.

You cannot be in a constant state of celebration, as it would not sustain the feeling of being fun and beautiful anymore.

Winning wouldn't be as exciting and fulfilling without the pain of defeat.

Even salty peanut butter is so much better with sweet jelly!

A life with only the good wouldn't actually be as fulfilling.

A rich, textured life is supposed to have both.

That's where life gets good, in this place of "both/and."

A day of laughter and tears and connection to others and your own soul is one of the greatest days you can have.

My wish for you is that you can embrace the "and."

That you intentionally allow yourself the gift of acceptance.

And from there stems the gift of growth.

That you feel the gift of determination and the gift of rest.

Another interesting and challenging duality concept deals with pain.

Pain shows us the true gifts in our life.

Physical pain shows us the gift of physical health.

Mental pain shows us the gift of mental ease.

Soul-filled pain shows us the gift of inner peace.

Pain is always a part of the human experience. Our soul isn't expecting us to live a life without pain. It's something that we are meant to experience, maybe so that the beauty of the joy and love and good is that much stronger. At some point in processing the pain, we might get to a point of trying on a new way of approaching it. Instead of continuing to seek the painful thoughts, and instead of shaming yourself for having painful thoughts, when you are ready, you might realize that you can try on a different way of thinking. Integrate these concepts as you feel ready.

You can always choose a new thought.

You can always choose a new path.

You can always choose new actions in response to your circumstances.

You can always listen to your heart-centered wisdom.

You can always choose to embrace the "and."

You are worthy of harmony within your body, mind, and soul.

You are worthy of embracing the duality of life.

You are worthy of inner peace.

You are worthy of the inner work to get to that place of intentionally living in alignment.

You are worthy of cultivating harmony as the peacekeeper of your soul.

Your inner light is your connection to your soul.

Embrace your innate radiance.

PART TWO

PART 2 SUMMARY:

Living Intentionally, Centered and Empowered in Harmony

Mantra: I honor my innate wisdom and true essence by coming home to myself and cultivating authenticity, inner peace, and harmony.

The theme of this section is empowerment. My intention for you in this section is to truly embrace that mindset matters. Your perspective can be shifted at your discernment, creating new feelings and choosing different actions that arise from that enlightened perspective. You can intentionally choose new, more empowering thoughts at any time.

Rediscovering your true essence, your gifts, your passions, and your values is a gift to yourself and to your loved ones and community. No matter how busy your life is right now, you deserve to carve out moments of time to go on the journey of reconnecting with the authentic you. You will feel more centered and empowered when you are connected to yourself.

Becoming the peacekeeper of your heart and soul is the journey of a lifetime. It requires true empowerment, self-awareness, and self-integrity. It is your birthright and worth every effort to create this state of being.

Embracing the gifts of harmony and duality is so empowering, and it is a continuation of the discussion of perspective shifts.

It's important to realize that life is not meant to be a bed of roses. Sometimes it requires stepping into your power as a generational pattern-breaker. There is actually so much freedom in knowing that challenges and hard times are a part of life, and when we honor ourselves and have this awareness, we are so much more equipped for the journey of those chapters.

Be gentle with yourself on these integrations, as these take time to integrate. Use the embodiment tools from Part 1 to allow these concepts to become a part of who you are and how you intentionally live your life. Know that just like the duality of life, this process of working on our mindset has its own ebbs and flows. There's excitement to explore, and then a dip, and hopefully a renewed interest to begin again. It's normal, and know that the growth doesn't leave you and is still happening.

When you combine all of these modalities, you are nurturing the sanctuary that you can create with your mind. That is an incredibly empowering skill set. Life gets to be played in a beautiful harmony of body, mind, and soul.

Let's move further into that part of our journey, the uplifting and enlightening process of connecting with our soul to truly shine our light.

PART THREE

Uplifted by Light—the Enlightenment

DESIGNED TO SHINE

The Beauty of Light: A Poem

See the light as glistening dots on the water,
Sparkling in a gorgeous concert of shimmer.
Angels dancing on the water.
Showing off for you,
Because you are watching.
Because they are beautiful.
Because they can.

See the light as sunrays breaking through the clouds in the sky,
Breaking through the leaves of a tree,
Breaking over the horizon in a sunrise.
Shining for you,
Because you are witnessing it.
Because they are beautiful.
Because they can.

See the light on the snow, glistening dots on the ground,
Brighter than you expected,
Reflecting and enhancing the beauty all around you.
Showing off for you,
Because you are a part of it.
Because it is beautiful.
Because it can.

See the light of a flame, flickering in the air,
Exuding a burst of different colors,
Delighted in its own spark.
Shining for you,

PART THREE

Because you are watching.
Because it is beautiful.
Because it can.

See the lights dazzling in the night sky,
Illuminating the darkness from so far away.
Shining so brightly for you,
Because you are witnessing it.
Because they are beautiful.
Because they can.

Now see the light inside of you,
Shimmering from your heart.
Delighted that you see it.
Shining for you,
Because you are a part of it.
Because it is beautiful.
Because it is you.

Now see your inner light,
Sparkling from your mind's eye,
Dancing with joy at its own brightness.
Showing you what's within you,
Because you are watching it.
Because of its beauty.
Because it is you.

Now see the light exuding from you.
Shining brightly from your crown of gold,

DESIGNED TO SHINE

Reflecting and enhancing the beauty all around you.
Illuminating your world,
Because you are witnessing it.
Because of its beauty.
Because it is you.

Now see the light exuding from your soul,
Illuminating your internal world,
Illuminating your external world.
Shining for all,
Because you are a part of it.
Because it is beautiful.
Because it is you.

10

The Light around Us

Whenever I walk toward the water of the ocean and I see the sparkling lights dance across the water from the sun in the sky, my heart always leaps. It's a vision that calls to my soul.

Light rays stream out from behind the clouds or peek through like angels through forest trees, and I see them as direct gifts from God and the universe. It's a little wave that says, "Hello, I'm here; I'm real."

That sparkling light on water has always made me think of angels dancing (and since I have the beautiful Lake Michigan close to my home, I seek out this vision and experience it as often as possible). Artists who can capture the essence of light in their art are awe-inspiring. The skill of photographers who can capture the beautiful effect of light on landscapes, in cities, and on people or animals is just incredible. It's the light that makes the picture. All of the interactions with light in nature, radiating and enhancing all that it touches, are a symbol of hope and love to me. It's not only highlighting the beauty around it. The light is beauty itself.

Light that is created by us as humans is beautiful too. Lighthouses are close to my heart, because my husband proposed to me in front of one, but they are also a metaphor for strength and hope, with their beacons of light guiding ships to a safe passage home. Flashlights are often used as a metaphor for how powerful it is to focus on something and to shine light in the dark. Carrying a torch or flame is another symbol of hope and love and even of unity, as is the amazing power of the flame that lights the next torch without diminishing its own light in any way. Candles and fireplaces in our homes add such a warmth and feeling of coziness. Think of all the candles in a cathedral or synagogue that only need one flame to start, and then they can all be lit up by that one initial flame. Isn't that really what we can do for one another when we come from a place of love? Isn't that what we can do when we shine our light, giving others permission and even empowering others to do the same?

Why are lights strung across a backyard so charming? Why are candles in a hurricane so alluring? Why does a firework display draw thousands of people every time they are set off? I believe that it's because of the light within us. They are all forms of celebration of our light. Our souls know it. It just resonates. It's fun to see things lit up. It's fulfilling to see people in their full light. It's how it's all meant to be.

By choosing to see the light around us, we give our minds proof that the light is there. Remember that our brains are naturally wired to see things negatively. This is an amazing protection mechanism developed through evolution to keep us safe. But it is our biggest challenge to see things in a better light. We have to look for the good. Choosing to see the light is a skill that can be strengthened by reframing our thoughts and by our intentional decision to look for it.

PART THREE

One of my favorite quotes on optimism says, "We can complain that rose bushes have thorns, or we can rejoice that thorn bushes have roses" (attributed to Abraham Lincoln). It's always about perspective. And our perspectives inform our beliefs.

Our beliefs are incredibly powerful. I believe that miracles are everywhere. Synchronicities are everywhere. Goodness is everywhere. Gifts of light are everywhere. We just have to choose to see them.

Let's go back to my story of being so sad and lonely with my two toddlers after having moved across the country. Two little miracles happened for me at that park, possibly in the same week. I already shared that quick interaction with the stranger passing by who changed my perspective for the better in an instant. His message was like a shooting star, a quick stream of beautiful light that stuck with me forever.

That park had even more light to shine upon me than just that beautiful perspective shift. Another life-enhancing moment was when I met a future lifelong friend at this park. She was from my hometown, and she had two little ones the same ages as mine. Just chatting with her felt like being home. And she graciously and quickly invited me into her world. Our oldest boys were only four years old when we met, and they have maintained an incredibly close friendship over the past sixteen years, even after they moved away in middle school, and now the boys are in college. She was a beacon of light sent to me by God and the universe. It wasn't just luck that I met her. It was a gift. And I am forever grateful.

These are the things that you want to look for in your life. Shift your perspective. Don't downplay synchronicity as just luck. They are gifts. They are light.

I believe in the availability of big miracles too. I love learning about them. I have faith in them. I trust that they are true and can happen. This feels like a true part of our existence to me. Our world and universe is vast and large, and we are spiritual beings, and it makes sense to me that miracles exist.

Seeing the light in other people is sometimes one of our greatest challenges, in our everyday lives and in the world at large. I know there are difficult people out there. I know there are people who are creating chaos. But for every negative story that our mind hears, we need to offset it with as much good as possible, as our brains always give more weight to the bad. It's a great practice to start seeking the good instead, and it will make your experience of the world a better place. When you decide to see the light of others, you will enlighten your own experience. Your energy will feel lighter. When you send out loving-kindness, you will receive more loving-kindness. When you send out light, you will receive more light.

Look for the light:

- Light of friends
- Light of family
- Light of our community
- Light of animals

PART THREE

- Light of spirituality
- Light of nature
- Light of art and creativity
- Light of music
- Light of the world

Integration: Seeing the Light around Us

Try looking at the world from your heart's perspective. Journal on these questions if that feels right.

1. Pick an area of your life or world about which you would like to feel better. Decide to create a new story that is more heart-centered and that allows you to see more light in others and in your world. Close your eyes. Put one or both of your hands over your heart. Ask yourself these questions: "How would I like to feel about this topic? In what way can I see the light around this situation? Who or what is shining here? How can I see more good?" Repeat the questions a few times, asking them in a few different ways, and anchor it in.

2. Pick an area of your life that you now realize is such a gift of light in your life. Reflect on the nuances of that gift and how it brings light to your life.

DESIGNED TO SHINE

3. Reflect on your favorite ways to experience light. How does it light you up?
   ....

4. Are there ways to incorporate more light into your life and the lives of others?

    This is such a powerful perspective and tool that will help you strengthen your ability to stay calm in the chaos and shine your own light as you see the light in others.

    You are worthy of the inner peace that the light brings.

    You are surrounded by light.

    Your acknowledgement of others' light only allows your light to radiate more.

11

The Light within Us

Do you know what your purpose is? Do you think of it as being connected to your inner light? In my interpretation, when you are in your purpose, your inner radiance gets to shine through. That's the yearning to fulfill, to connect with. It's what our soul wants. And sometimes, it's really hard to do it.

It's taken me my entire lifetime to decide to shine my light this brightly with a book. I needed to peel off several tough layers to figure out why this was so hard for me, especially when the phrase "shine your light" has resonated so deeply with me for my whole life. And no one was making me do this. I wanted to write a book, and I had to figure out what was holding me back from completing it. With a lot of digging, I realized that it starts with my story from certain aspects of my childhood. As a very young child (maybe three or four years old), I decided to stop speaking out loud, and I would only communicate through a whisper to my older sister. (Cheers to her for getting me the snacks I wanted.) In a house that was sometimes unpredictable and chaotic, that was a great safety play. If I couldn't be heard, I wouldn't be seen and I couldn't be the cause of any issues. While the family folklore of this time was that my whispering phase lasted only a couple of months, it's actually been at play in my subconscious and in my body for all of my life. It's a safety play. When I am quiet, I am safe. But that can get pretty lonely and disconnected. So it's a story that was running in the background of my life that I needed to let go.

"Speak your truth! Use your voice! Shine your light!" These phrases are blasted at us with the best of intentions, as even I am doing with this book. But they also can create so much resistance. The ego likes to tell us all the reasons not to do this. And for me, it wasn't just the discipline needed of getting out of my comfort zone. It was literally interpreted by my body as unsafe and truly scary.

While we do need more women to speak their truth and use their voice, it's not as simple as just deciding. First, we have to honor and create awareness about why it's so difficult for us in order to take those next steps forward. This is typically going to be caused by a variety of reasons, from our experiences to our personality types to our desires. We must honor how we are wired and what the right path is for us. As we are all unique individuals, this path to rediscovering our authentic selves and shining our light will look different for each of us.

When we have a shaky voice, racing heartbeat, and trembling hands before we speak to a crowd or give an important presentation, I wonder if that isn't a universal response to our basic need for safety. It's surprising to me how many of us struggle with that same fear. Being seen feels especially unsafe to some of us in our bodies. If that is you, I see you and I feel you.

However, it is the restoration of and reconnection with our inner light that is the path to our purpose, passion, and inner peace. This is our path to empowering ourselves. It is in our courage to share our gifts that our radiance is palpable.

PART THREE

And if many more people were living in their own soulful vision and fulfilling their purpose, wouldn't the world be that much more beautiful and bright?

So how do we get to know our inner light? Well, I don't believe our mind alone can figure it out. Our mind is very busy keeping us safe, and it does a great job of that, but that is also where the self-doubt creeps in. The self-doubt is the mind's attempt at safety.

The whispers of your heart and soul are your dreams and desires, messages that are worthy of being fulfilled. This is where you can pull back in the power of meditation and breathwork and slowing down, because the more you slow down, the more you can receive these internal messages of wisdom. Maybe the ideas come to you in the shower or when you first wake up in the morning. Wherever you can find your moments of a quieter mind is where your heart messages can come through more clearly. The calmness of the mind allows the inner voice to be heard. And your heart messages hold your inner light. This is the key to connecting with your highest vision.

In the process of writing this book, I signed up to be in a few group writing workshops. So many of the participants in those workshops said that they would never write a book, but they were attending because they loved to write. That situation made me curious. Was their inner critic talking them out of it because they have such high standards (and appreciation) of what good literature is and "should be" that they will not allow themselves to create at a level that might not live up to that? Will they regret at the end of their life that they didn't ever write a book? Or do they really just love writing for fun and their inner coach is guiding them to just live in their joy? It wasn't for me to know or judge, but it was an interesting situation to ponder, as neither is right or wrong. It's just about living in your truth. This awareness is the path to knowing if you are letting your light shine or not. Which voice is driving your decisions?

As you hear those messages from your heart and soul, question your doubts. Start to pay attention to your inner critic or saboteur, and when you hear that voice of fear, get in the habit of questioning the message. "Is that really true? What makes you think that?" This is where you pull in your inner coach or sage and choose more empowering thoughts.

Defining our purpose is also a big topic, as we put so much pressure on what it might mean. My perspective is that purpose doesn't have to be one thing or one definition of our life. It means many different things to different people. Purpose can also be many different things within one's life, changing over the seasons of our life. I know my purpose has changed with time. Within all the contexts, it is usually about fulfillment, passion, and a true calling.

It doesn't have to be our career, but for some lucky ones, it is.

It doesn't have to be one defining accomplishment of our life.

It doesn't have to be the same throughout our life.

Purpose can be seen as lighting up our soulful vision for this stage of our lives.

PART THREE

Once I became a stay-at-home mom, that was my biggest purpose. At the same time, I always had to have a side gig that wasn't related to my role as a mom. Over the almost two decades that I have been a mom, I had many other roles. I did a lot of volunteering at the school. I also did part-time consulting, and I sold health food, jewelry, clothing, skincare, and makeup. I started a small fashion styling business, and then I started a beauty business. While I didn't grow any of these into what society would deem a big success, they served their purpose for me. They were a success in providing what I needed at that time. I was trying on different hats of what interested me, using my creativity. I had a project to call my own outside of my mom role, which I loved, but I needed something else that was just for me. These projects fulfilled me by providing outside adult connection, fun, and service. These were all different sparks of my inner light.

All of these were stepping stones to my purpose today. The other business roles all had a smaller purpose of lighting up my life a bit along the way and allowing me to figure out what wasn't a good fit. Those experiences allow me to share more fully my inner light today.

Tapping into your purpose is a journey.

I truly believe in the perspective that the journey is the purpose!

Integration: Purpose Exploration

Start with asking yourself these questions:

- What does purpose mean to you personally?
- Is it a spiritual connection?
- Is it a life mission? A calling?
- Is it your career? Or how you spend your daily life?
- Is it applying your life lessons in some way?
- Have you felt that you had a different purpose at different times?

After defining what it means to you, then do some reflection on how you are living in your own purpose right now.

- Do you feel unfulfilled in some way?
- What would bring you fulfillment?
- Did you have a sense of purpose that you have lost?
- What is causing that?
- What would a new sense of purpose feel like to you?
- What would a new sense of purpose look like to you?
- How could you start to align more with your definition of purpose now?
- Does your body, mind, and soul feel connected to this idea?

PART THREE

Give yourself permission to not have to figure it out right away. Approach your interests with curiosity and playfulness, and see where it takes you.

Expect your answers to change over time. Very few of us know our one mission or our one purpose. Give yourself grace that it's okay to feel lost sometimes. The next chapter in this book will go further into honoring our season of life.

Another place that many of us can relate to is commitment in our careers. Career success comes from commitment, overcoming fear, and getting out of that comfort zone. It's okay to be uncomfortable. That's where we need to be in order to accomplish something big. Career success always comes with failure. Those failures are typically the greatest lessons of how to do things better, be better, create better. We have to test things out and be willing to fail in order to find our version of true success.

An important perspective on any journey is that we need to remember that all of these require rest. Overtraining physically can lead to injury. Excessive discipline with healthy choices can lead to eating issues and even disorders. Overworking leads to being overwhelmed, burnt out, and depleted creatively. We have to allow ourselves rest. Even God took the seventh day of creation to rest. It's a part of the process. It's the key to success in creating change. Our inner light often reveals itself the most clearly in a time of rest. Commitment, creation, rest. And trust.

Integration: Letting Go to Connect with Your Inner Light

In my experience, I realized that there was also a lot to let go of in the process of rediscovering your inner light.

It's the childhood stories that you don't even realize are still driving you.

It's the inner critic that is trying to keep you small and safe.

When you choose to let go of seeing yourself as a victim, you give yourself permission to be proactive in your own power.

Letting go of the judgment of yourself and others isn't easy. Often, our judgment of others is a reflection of something that we don't like about ourselves or is an area that we need to work on.

Another aspect is letting go of all the worry about what others will think. This drives all of us more than we'd like to admit, because being accepted as a part of a community is an inherent need. But what we don't realize is that when we keep ourselves playing small to avoid the judgment of others, we are not allowing ourselves to be aligned with our own needs. When we decide to release the fear of the judgment of others, we actually align ourselves with more people who are in the same place as us. People actually feel safer with us when we are connected to the truest version of ourselves. We create a tighter, more connected community when we are true to ourselves. We give other people permission to do the same.

We let go of the stories that no longer serve us.

We let go of the stories from our ego.

We let go of the fears of judgment.

PART THREE

We trust our inner knowledge, our heart messages, our soul's vision.

We allow in loving-kindness to both ourselves and others.

Then the rediscovery is happening.

You are standing in your own light.

You know who you are, and you honor that.

You will be calm in any chaos.

You will know inner peace.

What if finally believing that you are designed to shine is the permission slip you need to fully be the truest version of you?

How could you step into that?

You are worthy of being grounded in loving-kindness.

You are worthy of being centered in harmony.

You are worthy of being uplifted by light.

You are radiant.

You are light.

The light of your soul is within you, and it is meant to shine.

12

Honoring Your Season of Life

College drop-off is hard. It is surreal. It is sort of like birth, when one day you don't have a baby, and then the next day you do. It is surreal. The college drop-off is the other end of that. Your man-child lives at home one day, and the next day he doesn't (or beautiful daughters, for many of you). It's the natural flow of things in our society, and it's what we spend our parenting lives preparing them for. We can use that mindset perspective shift to lighten the load a bit and consider it a huge success. And it's still hard. Again, it's the duality of life: pride and melancholy, side by side. There is a space in time for this to be honored.

Connecting to your inner peace is challenging sometimes. Grief, loss, moves, job changes—they can all cause enough distress that we are actually changing as people. It's an identity shift, and change isn't peaceful most of the time.

But this is the paradox of life, because life is always changing. And we are always seeking inner peace.

Have you noticed that as the seasons of life change, we go through multiple identity shifts? Some shifts are exciting and expected, like our first jobs, marriages, or parenting. Some are so much harder than we thought they would be, including the exciting and expected ones. Some are brutal and unexpected, like the loss of loved ones. In many of them, we find ourselves asking, "What now?

PART THREE

What's next? Who am I in this season? How can I find inner peace when I feel so disconnected to what my life is right now?"

For me, my identity shifts have really been rooted in parenting. When I first became a mom, I struggled with finding my purpose. I know that sounds crazy, since logically it would make sense that my purpose was to care for my new baby. But I felt overwhelmed by the huge life shift. My husband and I had decided together that it also meant the end of my corporate career, but that was so much more nuanced once I was in it. It also meant the change in dynamic in my marriage of moving to a single income in that season. And then there was the repetition of the seemingly endless tasks at hand: feeding, changing diapers, sleeping, cleaning, on repeat. It was so hard to be in the middle of that season, as it feels so monotonous, and it was hard for me to see beyond the moment. I was just overwhelmed and lost, and in this massive identity shift that I was going through, I couldn't see the light.

I expressed this to a dear friend on a walk one day, as we pushed our baby strollers. I expressed how I felt like I had lost my purpose, that I needed to volunteer or something. And she said, "That's not how I see it. This is our purpose—being with our babies, doing the best job we can here. That's what we should be doing right now. We don't need to be doing anything else." And it was so interesting, that this clarity had not occurred to me on my own. Sometimes friends are little angel messengers too. Their words come out, and they don't even realize that their words will impact you for a lifetime. (Actually, we can choose to see that it's usually friends who are our angels all around us.)

DESIGNED TO SHINE

One day, when I was in the stage of being a mom to young teen boys, I sat next to a woman and her two-year-old child on an airplane. She was reading to her little one, trying to keep him from climbing the seats, and I was silently sobbing. She was reading a favorite bedtime story book that I used to read to my sweet baby boys years ago. I couldn't stop the tears from streaming down my face. I put on my sunglasses. I pretended that I was crying about the story from the book I was holding in my hands. And I was silently laughing at the absurdity of it. But it just hit me and I was suddenly so sad that those days were long gone. I love my teenage boys, but I loved my little toddler boys too. I loved them in a different way. And they are gone. It broke my heart to see and realize how much I missed them. I never realized in the moment that there was an ending, because the journey kept going. But I loved seeing the sweetness of that moment between a mother and her son, and I missed my little ones. And simultaneously, I realized how grateful I am that I am past the difficulties of that season, as I don't have to keep anyone from climbing in their seats anymore. It gave me a moment to appreciate how I love them as they are today and who they are now.

Several months later, a similar thing happened, when I saw a middle school boy in his baseball gear at our local grocery store. I spent years on the sidelines of baseball games. And while the games were long and the weather was often less than ideal, it was also the development of amazing friendships, among the parents and among the boys as well. It was an almost decade-long expe-

PART THREE

rience of highs and lows and celebratory dinners and consolation ice cream. It defined our family life and who was our community for years. It was so bittersweet to see this boy in that uniform and to know how special that time in our life had been. They were in it, and this stage was over for me. The emotions I felt included being sad that those days were long gone, but they also included appreciating that we had the beauty of the experience and again being grateful for being past the hard parts of it. (I don't miss cleaning white baseball pants!)

Going back to the college drop-off topic: sending your kids off to college (or seeing them move out, if college isn't in their plans) is obviously a monumental season of life. The process of letting go feels so unnatural for us (and often for them) and yet simultaneously the best thing for them, all at once. Your daily role is forever changed. For many parents, especially mothers, it can feel like a loss of a sense of purpose. Allowing yourself to feel whatever you are feeling around this transition can be a healthy process. I also invite you to allow in the perspective shift that you are a huge success and that you should be celebrated too.

This identity shift is true throughout life. It's true in our marriages, from the stages of becoming newlyweds to becoming parents to becoming empty nesters. It's true in the marriages that run their course over a shorter period of time, in the before, during, and after of that. It's true in our relationship with our parents, of being a kid, then coexisting as adults, and then becoming their caretaker. There's an identity shift in going off to college and becoming an adult, and missing home and high school and comfort. There are big moves to new cities, new states, and new countries. There are career changes. There are life-changing illnesses. The examples of identity shifts are truly endless. It always seems hard when we are in it, even when we love it. And for a while we might be relieved that those times are over, but often we will long for what was. It's such a conundrum of the human condition. So how do we move through it and stay true to ourselves? How can we honor the season we are in without getting stuck?

Sometimes, honoring the season may actually be the purpose. It's okay to be where you are now. It's so important to nourish yourself and honor the season of life that you are in and the seasons of life that you have been through. You can use that power of intentional thought work to find appreciation for what was, the appreciation for the good parts of now, and the appreciation for lighting a path to a bright future. Give yourself grace that moving through some of our more challenging seasons takes time. Give yourself compassion that this stage doesn't need to be compared to any other stage, and you can listen to your heart for how to move through it. I love gentle breathwork and meditations for self-compassion and self-care in this scenario.

When it is time, it's also powerful to reframe the thoughts around what is happening or has happened. Reflect on what lessons you have learned in each stage and embrace appreciation for the lessons. When I think back on that new mom version of me, I definitely did not feel like I was shining my light anywhere. But actually,

PART THREE

I was shining brightly for those sweet babies. And when I couldn't, I asked for help and allowed myself to be supported.

You may be in a season in which you don't want to shine brightly, or that shining at all sounds exhausting, and the idea of finding a lesson doesn't fit. Maybe you truly need to rest. Maybe you want to just find that inner calm and peace from a place of rest, without any pressure beyond that, and these tools will be perfect for that too. This is the heart-centered practice of self-compassion. This is gentle loving-kindness to ourselves. This is the ultimate in soul care, honoring this season of life. We can always choose to sit in the heaviness for a bit, and then we can always choose to see the light when we are ready. When you are connected to your soulful vision for this stage of life, you will know how to honor yourself. Sometimes the soul's vision is healing.

Even when you don't have the energy to shine, the light is there. That's when the love of others keeps a candle burning for you.

This is also where I would like to address the heartbreaking topic of tragedies or difficult illnesses or other really challenging parts of life. The common saying, "Everything happens for a reason," does not fully resonate with me. Tragedy being a part of a divine plan is hard for me to believe. Obviously, it is a part of our human experience, but I cannot get behind the message that certain people have to learn a lesson or that the angels needed that child back early. My perspective is that the human experience includes free will, and that is what often gets in the way of divine plans, especially now that mass shootings are a part of our society. Or environmental factors that have caused cancer to be on the rise over the last few decades. Natural disasters happen, but I do not believe the people who experience them were chosen for some reason to experience it. The entire community was not charged with learning a lesson.

What I do believe is that we can turn a tragedy into something good. The beauty of humanity's soul shows up in tragedy. That is where the true beauty of the human experience lies. We can take a huge challenge or tragedy and find the silver lining and create meaning and messages from that space.

We have all heard of PTSD (post-traumatic stress disorder), but have you ever heard of the post-traumatic growth phenomenon? There are examples of this everywhere, like former athletes or soldiers who lose a limb and become paralympic athletes. Or people turning their lives completely around after near-death experiences. Many fundraising foundations are created out of tragedy (such as the many different type of cancer foundations, Alzheimer's foundations, parents against drunk drivers and gun violence—the list is endless). These incredible, inspiring stories of people choosing to do something meaningful with a tragedy that they experienced is so admirable. And it is a way to honor that person or event in their lives that may have experienced tragedy. It's honoring life. It is honoring the season. And it is humbly shining their light.

My own version of this has always been to look for the better way, the better perspective, and the path of growth. Growing up

PART THREE

in a home with considerable anger management issues, some physical violence, and mental victimhood all around, there were a lot of patterns that could have been repeated in my adult life. Yet somehow, I always knew there was a better way, and I chose a different path.

Life is not always positive or sunny, nor should we pretend it is. But the inspiration is always available to us of using the power of mindset and intentional living to move forward and ask ourselves these questions: How can we make things better? Where can we find the light behind the cloud, the silver lining? What are the gifts in our challenges?

Navigating midlife is its own major curveball. Since I am officially in it, I see the struggles of my peers as each of us tries to make our way. Answering the question of what's next is relevant to so many circumstances within this stage. In addition to the big ones like divorce, career burnout, and empty nesting, there is also the common occurrence of realizing that time is ticking, and we wonder if we are living the life we were meant to live. If you are in the middle season of life, the combined pressures of parenting your older children and caretaking of aging parents, or any other scenario that pulls you in two or more directions, can weigh on your well-being. It scatters your thoughts into the opposing ideas that you don't have time to do anything for yourself and that you are running out of time. It weighs on our inner peace. It weighs on our desire to shine our light.

In the process of pondering the meaning of our current stage of life, the first thing we need to remember to do is to find ourselves in it. We lose ourselves without intentionally doing so. We are showing up for everyone else so much that we don't have time to show up for ourselves. But as we discussed in the earlier chapter, "Be the Peacekeeper of Your Heart and Soul," when we do not make the time for self-care and soul-care, we become depleted mentally, physically, emotionally, and spiritually. And when we are depleted, we are not showing up for those we love with the energy we want to give to them. Take back that control through the power of an abundance mindset. Know that you are worthy of taking care of yourself too. Know that you will show up better for everyone whom you are trying to take care of when you take care of you. Remember that thoughts become our reality, and we can choose more empowering thoughts anytime.

From there, consider what you can use as inspiration in your own life now that you can celebrate. It may mean creating more curiosity about the season of life you are in and what you want from it. It may be about digging deep within you to find out what you need from this season of life. How can you honor yourself? How can you honor this season?

PART THREE

Integration: Honoring This Season

What would be an aligned way to live my life in this season to honor my soul and allow myself to show up and shine? In what way can this season be a season of light?

When you have practiced integrating mindset work and embodiment work (breathwork, meditation), you will most likely be in a much better place to handle the chaos when it comes your way. And we all know it's coming in some form and at some point. So why not prepare ourselves to be in a better position of inner peace to tap into for the next wave? Why not prepare ourselves to be the calm in the next storm of chaos?

Remember to compare mindset and embodiment work to fitness. You don't want to wait to start your exercise routine after you've been hospitalized for heart issues. You work out to hopefully reduce your chances of those heart issues. Prepare your mind and body for the next wave.

Remember to always give yourself compassion. Approach your season with loving-kindness. We can always choose a new thought. Life gives us the gifts of each new day, and each new moment, to choose again.

Calmness of the mind is one of the beautiful tools of wisdom. Embrace your wisdom. Embrace this season of your life. Embrace your inner peace. Embrace the gift of new beginnings and choosing again.

DESIGNED TO SHINE

Journaling on the above questions can be a powerful practice to tap into your own internal answers. Of course, journaling after breathwork and meditation is the most powerful combination!

You are worthy.

You are enough, right now, exactly in this season.

You are made of light.

You are meant to shine in every season of life.

13

Choosing Joy

"I'm definitely having a lot of fun!" This was my immediate default response when I first started my life coaching training and we were asked to rank each area of our lives, one of which was "Fun and Leisure." "Of course I'm making time for fun. Joy is a priority for me!" I was very confident in this response. I am a happy person, so that had to mean I was choosing joy. Then I sat with it for a few minutes, and this voice in the back of my head said, "Do you have fun? In what way are you prioritizing that?" I hadn't enrolled in the dance class I had been talking about joining—for years! I didn't take the piano lessons I wanted to take, even though every time I drive by the house that offers piano lessons my eyes fill up with tears. I didn't make reservations for high tea for my birthday. I did enroll in a lot of personal development classes that I love learning through, but was that fun and joyful?

A balanced life, a life of harmony, prioritizes the right amount of fun and allows you to choose joy. A balanced life should feel good to your soul. I started to become curious about how I could be intentional about choosing more joy.

Are you waiting for joy to find you or to spontaneously happen to you?

What if one of the most important lessons of heart-centered living is to choose joy in our everyday life?

What if joy can be found in the micro-moments of our daily life?

What if joy is a decision?

What if tapping into that joy was actually of service to yourself because it has a ripple effect that becomes a service to your world?

Let's revisit my love of tea (because I love tea and love talking about tea). There is something about having tea that makes me profoundly happy. Was I a part of the British royal family in a past life? A tea farmer? Where did this love come from? It wasn't like it was some big part of my childhood. The first time I experienced the beauty of a true high tea service was a graduation party in high school—and I fell in love with the entirety of the experience. I have traveled overseas and made going to tea a priority. I spent my fortieth birthday celebration gathering friends and having afternoon tea (which joyfully turned into dinner and an evening out, but I digress). I have loved going to holiday tea with my sister-in-law and niece, which motivates me to want to make time for this in my life more often. And I have a cabinet full of tea options to bring this happiness into my daily life, and while it's not the same, it does help me to remember the feeling of how much I love a full tea service. And that is the secret of choosing micro-moments of joy in our daily lives. We want to create experiences similar to the bigger moments of joy. When we generate these feelings in our bodies, we align more closely with our true selves. When we are aligned with our true selves, we show up in the world with better energy. And that is a service, to yourself, to your loved ones, and to the world. Listen to what lights up your soul. Make it a priority. Let it be easy.

PART THREE

Music and dancing have always been a part of who I am. Some of my favorite childhood memories are the many late nights spent at our summer cottage, dancing in the dark with my sister and cousins (the same ones with whom I climbed the gorge). The light from the boathouse was swirling with the evening summer bugs, and it served as our spotlight as we made up routines to "Eye of the Tiger" and many other great anthems of the eighties. Our shadows would dance on the boathouse with us, and our laughter would move across the lake water. The grass was cold beneath our feet, but we were blissfully sweaty from dancing and laughing. That recollection is so clear because I was in a state of joy, fully present in the moment.

I also loved taking ballet and tap and jazz dance. I loved playing the piano in harmony with my dad. It was a connection point for us in an otherwise complicated relationship. As I mentioned, I can't drive by the local piano lesson studio without my eyes filling up with tears. I have always been moved to tears by music. I cry at every live musical and concert. But that emotion isn't one of sadness. It's my body's recognition of something I love speaking to my soul.

When I feel disconnected or in a down mood, my favorite solution is a little dance session. If I am about to get on an important call and I know I will be sitting for a while, but I want to show up with great energy, the best thing I can do is hold my own private dance party. The ways that I bring dance and music into my daily life is truly so simple: kitchen dance parties, and creating good playlists for cooking or walking or getting ready for the day. I could plan to attend more live concerts. I could sign up to take adult hip-hop classes and piano lessons again. I can decide to incorporate more of the joy of music in my life.

You can decide to be in this state of joy too. One way that I recommend implementing this into your life is to start a joy practice, similar to a gratitude practice. Start your day with it. What brings you joy first thing in the morning? Your cozy blanket? Your coffee? Your cute dog waking you up? The songs of the cardinals outside your window? Your beautiful children? Could you have a breakfast dance party and get the whole family out the door in a joyful mood? Could you find ways to incorporate a joy practice throughout your day? What would you bring in that would be your "cup of tea," so to speak? What makes your heart sing? What kind of energy does that idea create in your body? How does the possibility of it make you feel? How would it make you feel to actually be doing it?

The majority of us do not prioritize remembering to play and enjoy life as an adult. We spend so much of our time focused on how we can create success. We want success at work. We want our kids to be successful. We want our relationships to be successful. All of these are great aspirations in theory. But we get confused about it when we try to live up to society's version of success without even stopping to think about whether or not it will make us happy when we get it. It all creates so much pressure, and it's not actually the point of life. The point of life is to love and be loved and create some joy along the way.

Are you feeling resistance to this idea? The negative self-chatter might be saying that fun and joy are silly. Or that it's child's play.

PART THREE

Or even that you aren't worthy of making the time for it, as you have too many serious responsibilities. Or that it must be nice to have that kind of time. When any of us let this voice be our driving voice, we create more disconnection within ourselves. We are worthy of fun and joy. Our inner peace and joy are not silly, insignificant things. They are actually everything.

Starting a joy practice could look like deciding to start to shift some of the time spent thinking about the ways to be successful and instead making a slight adjustment to thinking about how to make things fun. Focus on how to play again. Focus on how to create joy. This will take an intentional adjustment in thinking, as some of that resistance is bound to come up in the background of your thoughts. That fear of not doing enough or not being enough is persistent. Witness those thoughts, and ask, "What part of that is true? How can I reframe some of those thoughts to come from love and add more joy?" We've all heard the saying, "Where attention goes, energy flows." Our brain is going to create more of what we focus on. Like a flashlight, we can direct our beam of light on what we want to create more of in our life. Light your path for joy.

Just like everything in life, what brings you joy is unique to you! When you start leaning into what makes you happy, it reconnects you to your values, purpose, and vision. It fills you up just thinking about it. It's not something that you have to go and find. It's just something to rediscover from your intuition and align your life to include more of it.

Integration: Creating a Joy Practice:

Create the space for joy in your life. Explore what sounds like fun! Take the time to answer these questions for yourself:

- What did you love to do as a child?
- What makes you happy today?
- What do you feel is missing and could make you happier?
- What are three things you could do to instantly lift your mood?
- What are your favorite things to do?
- What is your favorite hobby?
- Have you ever been so involved in something from a place of joy and fun that you lost a sense of time? What about that experience was so joyful?
- Is there a way to incorporate some of that experience into your life today or this week or this month?
- What moves you to tears from a place of love?
- What's something you've always been curious about?
- What was your favorite class and why?
- What skills would you like to master?
- What does creativity look like for you?
- What would you love to create from a place of fun and joy?

PART THREE

Further Ways to Choose Joy to Create Change and Overcome Fear

Why do we wait until we hit rock bottom to create change? Why wait for loss or pain or illness, and then change? That is such an interesting characteristic of our typical mode of operation. When we finally feel bad enough or make enough disempowering decisions, then we decide we have to do something about it. Then we decide we can't live that way anymore. What if we reframed this whole process in our lives?

Why not choose to create change out of joy and inspiration? What if we decided to enhance our lives, no matter how great they are right now, to make them even better? We can start with where we are today and really take the time to reflect on how we can enhance our daily life. We can decide to be proactive in our pursuit of health and happiness. Our approach to life can be a journey of choosing joy.

The decision to be proactive in choosing joy to create change is another example of how powerful we can be when we use intentional thought work. You might have these positive conscious thoughts that say, "Yes, I want to be happy and healthy." But when we don't take the time to tap into our subconscious to create the change, our body and habits take over. It's not really a lack of cognitive willpower and desire. It's your subconscious taking charge and pulling you back into its comfort zone. The decision to be proactive needs to be supported through our daily practices of alignment, integration, and mindset work. This is intentional living.

As we discussed in an earlier chapter, purpose does not have to be a goal or destination to achieve. It is a way of being. It brings joy.

Does fear or judgment also keep you from experiencing joy? Joy is often on the other side of fear that I have felt often (for example, writing a book, launching a podcast, and so on). Sometimes joy will require you to step out of your comfort zone and surprise yourself.

Hiking on a glacier had never been a bucket list item for me. I don't like to be cold. I don't know why we would want to walk with ice picks on the bottoms of our boots. I have no idea why we would take an amazing trip to Argentina in the summer months and still pack winter clothes for the glacier outing. I didn't see the intrigue. And yet, let me tell you, it's one of the most amazing things I've ever done. It was so beautiful. It was such an incredible experience. That brought me joy. And I was way outside of my comfort zone.

Writing this book has also been a journey of stepping outside of my comfort zone. And I know that the success is really in the journey of doing it, and then following through and completing it. The real success is showing others that we can shine our light whenever we decide to, at any age, for whatever reason is driving you. That brings me joy. And it's way outside of my comfort zone.

What joy awaits you outside of your comfort zone?

PART THREE

Wholehearted Joy

Wholehearted joy is the most powerful way to be present in the moment. Wholehearted joy is connected to a life well-lived. It is the perfect combination of being grounded, centered, and radiating light.

The feeling for me of wholehearted joy ties back to the power of grounding. Anytime I am at a beach, it honestly resonates in my soul. The right music brings tears to my eyes within a few notes. Dancing can make me cry happy tears too. That wholehearted joy is a connection to nature, to music, to my heart and soul.

When I was a kid, my favorite thing to do was dance. That's all I remember—music and dance (and maybe a slight obsession with makeup; but I digress). My dream was not that of being in the lead dance role. I honestly wanted to be a backup dancer on all of the videos on MTV back in the eighties. I wanted to show my talent and explode in joy and life and fun without all eyes being on me. This is an interesting observation, too, in self-knowledge. Our society tells us to want the lead, the limelight—and I truly have never wanted that. I might have wanted to want it—do you know what I mean? Because society regards it in high esteem, it seemed like it should be the goal. But that was never what would bring me joy, and I knew it without a doubt.

Where does joy have a place in your soulful vision? Can you see the possibilities to bring more joy into your life? To me, wholehearted joy is bigger than happiness. It feels more like fulfillment.

Obviously, when we are joyful, our light automatically radiates out of us and all around us. While joy and calm are not typically associated with one another, when you think of it from your soul's perspective, they go hand in hand. When you reconnect with joy, you reconnect with your inner peace. That's when you are radiant. That's what's calling to us. That's where we are meant to live. That's when we shine.

Integration: Wholehearted Joy

How can you let joy wash over you today?

How can you see the simple beauty of something in your life today and really feel it in your body?

What is most real and true?

Remember to let in the beauty of today.

Be. Here. Now.

How can you choose more peace and ease today?

Who are you being in this moment, on this day?

Be. Here. Now.

When you step into what brings you joy, you are shining your light.

Go play. Find your joy.

In peace.

In joy.

In your soulful vision.

You are inherently worthy.

You are more than enough.

You are radiant light.

14

Shine in Your Soulful Vision

I've questioned myself countless times along the way, both in writing this book and in my business journey. "Is this the right path for me? Is this what I'm meant to be doing?" And when I pray or meditate on this topic, and I'm really feeling the big pull of insecurity, I ask for signs. Over the past year, I've gotten some really beautiful feedback from the universe. But recently, I decided to take a big risk and ask for something super specific.

I said to God, angels, and the universe, "If this is what I am supposed to be doing, I want a big sign this time. I am asking for a bouquet of flowers, not from my husband. Not a picture of flowers, a real-life bouquet." And wouldn't you know it, the flowers were delivered four days later. When I got the text from my friend who is a florist that she had a delivery for me, tears streamed down my face. And I shook my head yes, and said "Okay, God. I got it. Thank you."

The lesson here? Trust yourself. Ask for support when you need it. And trust God, or the universe, or whatever the divine looks like for you. I've had to go on this path to feel the fear, feel the self-doubt, and choose to show up and shine anyway so that I could share how to actually follow through and do it. My soul has a vision, and it is my job and choice to live intentionally and step into it.

Many people have asked me what inspired me to write a book. It wasn't a big epiphany. It was more like a gentle calling, a knowing, an intention. My inspiration is literally this chapter, as I want you to shine in your soulful vision. I believe everyone has their own unique inner light, their own unique vision of what their gifts are to share with the world. And I wanted to give my readers, you, the permission slip to get started. Because there are infinite possibilities for each of you. And you just need to follow your heart and soul and start. You just need to take the leap to include more of your passions in your life. This is in fact the point of life.

When it comes to your life, what would make you truly happy? What do you really want your life to be about? What would you like the next three years to look like? What about at the end of your life? What does that version of you hold with such awe and appreciation and gratitude that you cultivated?

On the journey you've taken by reading this book, and any other part of your journey to greater self-awareness and seeing more joy and light in your life, is the answer more available to you?

You already have all of the answers.

Your intuition and inner knowledge are right there inside of you, waiting for you to trust them and invite them into the aligned creation of your life, into the creation of your soulful vision.

What if you are so powerful that you can create exactly the life you want if you just got out of your own way?

What might change if you put that power and trust into your inner knowledge to let your soulful vision come to life?

What if you asked your heart to lead you there?

Your greatest purpose is to be living in your soulful vision for the stage of life you are in. The identity shifts of our life do sometimes make this hard. We need to approach those shifts with lov-

PART THREE

ing-kindness, giving ourselves grace, as well as with heart-opening curiosity. When we wonder, "What's next?" we can lessen the feeling of being stuck or lost with the more empowering mindset framework of fun and play and limitless possibilities.

Your greatest gift is your inner light. Your greatest wisdom is found in inner peace. You are the only one who can decide that you want to allow it in. We are all designed to shine, but it is the intention and integration that make it happen.

Do you hear the inner voice that tries to downplay this? Do you hear a voice that says, "It might be true for a lot of people, but maybe that's not true for me"? When you hear this, go back to listening to your heart. Let your heart and soul take the lead. Use your inner coach, knowing she is always available to you.

Marianne Williamson's book *A Return to Love* was released in the early nineties, and it was somehow on my radar right away. This book, and especially the famous words about shining your light because you are a child of God *(REFERENCES: BOOKS THAT WERE INSTRUMENTAL IN MY PERSONAL DEVELOPMENT JOURNEY AND ARE INFLUENCES ON MY WORK),* just stopped me in my tracks. I read it over and over, and I have gone back to it countless times over the years. It hit me in my soul. I knew deep down that it was true. All this time since that initial reading, I have been leaning into it—integrating that knowledge, embodying that belief. I hope you believe that you can do it too.

We can all think of famous people who stepped into their greatness. We can all think of people in our communities or even people who we are lucky enough to know personally who have stepped into their greatness. They make a difference in the world by leading with love. They have stepped into their gifts, into their soulful vision.

Allow in the possibility that this can be your way of being too. It doesn't have to be big. It doesn't have to bring you fame. It just has to resonate with your soul. This can be your way of being. This is you. You just have to decide. And act.

This is where we have to live and breathe by intention. We have to live in intention. This is true integrity, to be fearlessly authentic, to keep our promises to ourselves, to navigate continually back to alignment, integration, and mindset. It is stepping into our self-belief and making our higher vision our reality. It is choosing to embody all that we want to be. It is realizing that when we choose to shine, we are stepping into all that we are meant to be. We are enlightened. We are home.

Integration: Your Soulful Vision

Some reflection questions to ask yourself about your soul's vision would be the following:

- What are the whispers from your soul that you are ready to hear?
- What is not only your ideal life but your aligned life?
- If your soul painted this picture of you empowered by your innate radiance, what would that scene look like?

PART THREE

> Where would you be? Who would you be with? What would you be doing?
> - How can you mix your current reality and open the door for your soulful vision?
> - How can you create this vision two years from now?
> - How can you create this vision two months from now, and six months from now?

Generate some short-term actions that the future version of you needs you to start doing today.

What about when resistance pops up? How will you manage yourself in your follow-through during those questioning moments? Yes, we know the dip is coming. The inner critic isn't going away, it's just a little less powerful than it used to be. Be prepared to support yourself to commit to your visions. Call on your inner coach or your inner sage or your inner cheerleader—whatever resonates for you. She has your back. Just call her in. Have a chat. (Of course, this is the beauty of a coaching relationship too.)

It is incredible that when you do start to put yourself out there, in any format, others around are inspired, while some are triggered. Yes, some people who are not in a growth mindset might start talking about you behind your back, saying those things your ego says too: "Who is she to do that? Who does she think she is? She needs to stop." People might say that. But you know what? Who cares? That doesn't matter. It doesn't matter what they say. What is the worst thing that can happen from that? Literally nothing besides a bruised ego. You can let it go. Whip out that energy protection bubble, bless and release the negative chatter, and do your thing. Focus on the people you are inspiring and serving. Focus on the people who need you. Time is finite. Your time to shine is now. Lean into it.

God, the angels, and the universe want you to fulfill your soulful vision. Your life's journey is to learn how to move past the chaos and the negative thinking. We often create these situations in our lives or even in our thoughts, because that is what we are used to. You can use the tools in this book to overcome that. Our thoughts create our reality. You can choose to be grounded in loving-kindness, centered in harmony, and uplifted by light, all at the same time. You can choose to live an abundant life.

15

Abundance Is Success of the Soul

As you've gotten to know me in this book, you will not be surprised to learn that my interpretation of abundance is not the norm. As I've used this term more and more, I have seen that it brings up a lot of money stories from people, with a potentially negative connotation and so much resistance.

When you think of abundance as a person, who do you think of? Oprah? Other celebrities or the super wealthy? Do you ever think of Mother Teresa? With intentional thought reframing, I invite you to consider that abundance is not just about money. It's about the soul behind the attitude of service and love. And for some, like Oprah, that comes with monetary abundance. But there are plenty of wealthy or successful people who don't fit the vibration of true abundance.

That societal definition of success, like career and money success, is often associated with striving for abundance. Most of us go through life with this focus on what we are getting or achieving, or where we are going, before we focus on *who we are being*. This is how we end up being overwhelmed, even when we achieve society's version of success. It still doesn't feel like an abundance mindset, and instead it feels like a permanent state of being overwhelmed because it's never enough. It's a scarcity mindset. There are more goals to hit and more money to make.

Several celebrities have been quoted talking about how fame and success are not the cure for happiness that you think it will be. Many successful business people struggle with this; they have huge monetary and career success, yet they realize that it all feels empty in that state of burnout.

When you are overwhelmed, you don't allow space for true abundance, no matter how much money you earn. True abundance is the opposite of this.

Abundance is truly the success of the soul.

Now, don't get me wrong. An abundance of money is a great thing too, as it is a tool for many wonderful things. Yes, you can treat yourself and enhance your experiences with money. You can also do more good things for the world when you have an abundance of money. And when you do good things with it, with a generous heart, that is also success of the soul.

Money is not abundance itself. That is a society-driven interpretation that has stories written all over it. We all have money stories, making it good or bad, enviable, and even unattainable. But money itself is actually a neutral tool onto which we are projecting stories. And this is separate from real abundance.

Abundance in nature evokes visions of flower fields and fertile crops, oceans and mountains. Abundance in spirituality evokes visions of infinite love and light and inner peace. So how does that relate to us? How can we empower ourselves to incorporate it into our mindset? How can we embody it and actually manifest our higher vision? How can we create abundance in our daily life?

PART THREE

An abundance mindset is about an abundance of love, an abundance of nature, an abundance of beauty, an abundance of impact and influence, an abundance of generosity. It's an abundance of gratitude, an abundance of peace, an abundance of fulfillment, an abundance of light. Abundance is often spiritual. Abundance is an overflow of ease. Abundance is being lit up from within. When you approach life with the viewpoint that there are infinite and abundant possibilities, you can truly lead with love and light up the world.

In a session with one of my excellent and intuitive coaches, she noticed that I held my corporate success with high energy, and my future success with my own coaching practice with high energy, but that I was belittling my role and success for the in-between parts: the motherhood days and years. And yet that has been my most fulfilling role in life, the most purposeful role in life: raising other human beings to be good people, to be kind and brave, confident and humble, committed and balanced. As we all know, that is no small feat. And while I am biased in believing my parenting went well and blessed in that I was given the opportunity to parent two incredible human beings, I somehow made light of it in my mind. It didn't hold the same weight as career success (which is an old story in our society that I wasn't really aware that I was adopting). I had bought into the idea that parenting wasn't about me and therefore wasn't the same as career success somehow. And yet, it was so much about me: being a caretaker, being a role model, being a nutritionist and educator and nurse and counselor—being fully present as a parent. What an incredible role. What an incredible purpose. What an abundance of success in the everyday things that are actually the most important things. My coach beautifully reminded me that I should celebrate that.

Let's bridge that gap in your life and hold up what you are not giving yourself enough credit for: not just equal in energy to career success and community success, but higher, greater, and more purposeful. What deserves to be celebrated? Where do you already shine, but you have been downplaying it? Where do you already have abundance?

A great place to start is with who you care for. If you are not a parent, you are still a caretaker of some kind: your career and clients, your friends, your parents, your community, your animals, your garden, your environment. Your caretaking holds the same energy, the same greater meaning and purpose. Let's celebrate that.

Look back on all the areas of your life that we have explored. Celebrate your strengths, your gifts, your values. Celebrate your gratitude practice, your joy practice, your season of life. Celebrate your light. Let your light shine brightly if you are ready. Let your light shine softly if that's what speaks to your inner peace.

You have to be intentional. You have to decide. You can choose to create the abundance that is available all around you.

I took a long pause while writing this book, and I think it had a lot to do with embracing the spirituality of my message. Again, I was waiting for someone to come along and knight me as a spiritual thought leader! But the fact of the matter is that I had to trust myself and get out of my own way. I had to own that my spirituality has been one of my strongest pillars in my whole life, and that is a part of my light and my life story. I had to tap into that highest version of myself once again, like I shared in my introduction of this book and my vision of my future self. I had to claim my message, be intentional, and see the abundance in the power of sharing.

This is my message for you: that you can tap into that highest version of yourself too. See how your higher self is showing up and how you implement your desired actions. Meditate on that vision and ask yourself that. Guidance will come when you open yourself up to it.

Integration: Abundance

Set aside some meditation and journaling time. Ask your heart, and ask your soul:

- What does true abundance mean to me?
- Where do I need to allow more abundance in my life?
- What else is missing?
- What is a soulful vision of my life?
- How can I live out that soulful vision today?
- Where can you create the space in your day and in your week to allow yourself to open up?

I know you might tell yourself that you do not have time for a morning routine. But can you throw a journal and pen in your purse, and write out some thoughts while you are waiting in the carpool line or coffee line? Or before the soccer game starts, or before your next meeting? Can you go for a walk during one of your phone calls? Can you put reminders in your phone to take deep breaths and become centered for one minute? Can you create a positive mantra to say to yourself that would energize you each day? What actions would resonate for you to make each day a little more nourishing, a little more aligned?

A.I.M. for Your Vision

Alignment. Integration. Mindset: A.I.M. I like to use this acronym as a tool to remind myself how I want to show up for my greater vision. I can run my feelings and actions through these three pillars to answer questions I might have in my everyday life. These are the keys that you can use to design your life to be connected to your vision. It starts in the now, in the enlightened awareness of being aligned, in the embodied action of integration, in the empowered perspectives of mindset work.

This is the method I created for myself and for my clients, and for all of you.

Know that if you commit to spending time each day to your gratitude and growth, through the awareness and integration practices recommended throughout this book, you can design your life to be exactly what your heart desires it to be.

It's all here for you. A.I.M. for your light-filled vision, and abundance will become a part of you.

PART THREE

PART 3 SUMMARY:

Living Intentionally, Uplifted and Enlightened by Light

Mantra: I nurture the inner sanctuary of my soul.
I illuminate my inner and outer world with my innate radiance.
I am uplifted by the abundant light in the world.

This section is where I saved the best for last, although it is impossible for me to talk about any part of life without bringing in the soul connection. This is the beginning of the journey of getting to know our soul and our inner wisdom, embracing that there is not a final destination of pure enlightenment for most of us. This is also about our interconnection with each other and a Higher Power. It's about taking the awareness of a greater connection to spirituality we gain along the way and integrating it into our current reality.

My intention for you in this section is to remind you of all the light in our lives and in this world. There is so much good all around you. There is so much good within you. You now have the awareness to focus on that and choose to cultivate more of it. You've hopefully heard the saying, "Where attention goes, energy flows." Living intentionally with a desire to add more light to our world means choosing to focus on the good.

Think of how a candle doesn't dim itself by lighting up other candles. It just creates more light. You can do that too.

DESIGNED TO SHINE

I interpret the discussion of manifestation in that we have to take action to create the desires of our heart and soul. If we are just trying to align ourselves by "feeling good" and then waiting for it to arrive, manifestation is going to be disappointing. The universe needs us to act with intention. Yes, we want to align with those desires, and then we need to integrate them through new decisions and behaviors. And that is when our light can shine the brightest.

Your purpose and passions, strengths and values, are a unique combination and gift to the world. No one else can or will make the impact that you have the potential to make, because your imprint is uniquely yours. You have the free will to choose how to play with that, how to let it flow in with ease and joy. Allow in grace to know that your purpose changes and grows as you change and grow. Remember that the journey is also the purpose.

Honor who you are at each stage of your life. Honor the changes and the times that you need to rest. Honor the season, and when you are ready, honor the next chapter by deciding to be in it. When times are dark, look for the light.

Seek joy in the present moment. Be devoted to a childlike curiosity, and find ways to be creative, expressive, and playful. Don't underestimate the importance of this to your genuine happiness. When you step into what brings you joy, you are shining your light.

Seeking true abundance is seeking success of the soul. This is the journey of our lifetime. I think this is actually the point of our human experience: connecting the mind, body, and soul to their source.

PART THREE

Bringing the embodiment practices and the perspectives of empowerment into your everyday life are intertwined with your ability to live a more enlightened life. As always, be gentle and remember that the ebbs and flows are a part of the process, a part of life.

Most importantly, nurture the inner sanctuary of your soul. This will illuminate your life.

Closing Words: The Journey of Living Intentionally to Discover Your Inner Light

When I started writing this book, I didn't know it would have the three-part structure that reflects the body, mind, and soul. I love so much that it turned out this way, as I have always believed that all three of those parts of us need to be cared for equally. It's honoring the holy trinity within us. The disconnected feelings we go through in life typically happen when we are not attending to one or more of these areas.

If someone asked me what I would want everyone in the world to know, of course it would be the message of this book: You are designed to shine. You are meant to light up your world with your own unique inner light. You are meant to lead with your heart and lead with love. You are meant to face the chaos of the world with an inner peace and graceful strength, connected to your true essence and light. Your purpose is to be living in your soulful vision in the here and now, and to share the love that comes with that gift.

I know it's hard. There's so much self-doubt, imposter syndrome, judgment, fear of failure, fear of success, the stories of it being not the right time or that it's too late. It's scary to take a leap. Sometimes, it's scary to dip your toe in. The incredible journey of facing your fears and the growth you will go through is worth every uncomfortable step.

The most impactful way I have found to release your fears, reduce the state of being overwhelmed, and improve your stress levels is to do the embodiment practices (Part 1 of this book). These all serve to help you reset your nervous system and increase resilience. When this starts to improve, then you'll be able to hear those message from your heart and soul more clearly. That's when clarity and peace and purpose come in.

It's been an interesting lesson even in writing this book, because I had to learn another layer of self-trust in my message. I wrote this book because it was a vision that I had from my higher self. And yet, in completing this book, I was once again waiting for that permission. I wanted someone to come along and knight me as a spiritual thought leader, and then I would be worthy of completing the book. I discovered there is no such governing body or certification that I could earn that would give me that. It's in the action of writing the book and getting it out into the world that I can start to own that title.

I am a different person than who I was two years ago at the beginning of this journey. I'm more confident and clear in my purpose. I'm more embodied in who I am as a person and in my daily rituals,

PART THREE

which have strengthened my connection to my inner wisdom and inner peace. I know myself so much more deeply, and for that, I am forever grateful that I did this.

What are my daily rituals? I almost always find time for meditation, and in certain seasons, I will meditate morning and night. The morning meditation usually incorporates breathwork. I have seasons in which I will journal daily for a month or two at a time, and then I might take a break from that for a bit. The rest of the ways that I can nourish myself are always in flow; different exercise routines, changing nutritional paths, trying other modalities and support. I check in with myself as I go, and when I am feeling off, I seek out what rings true for me at the time that would be helpful. The further along this path I have gone, the better I have become at knowing what my body, mind, or soul might need. The same will be true for you.

Know this: Your fears and self-doubt are not something that will go away, but you can give yourself compassion and confidence to take action anyways.

You can make the decision to integrate daily practices to connect your body, mind, and soul and choose to be empowered, even if it's uncomfortable at first. Just as fitness needs to be a part of how we spend our time for the duration of our life in order to be healthy and thriving, so do mindset and soul connection practices.

It's the key to a fulfilling life.

It's the key to your resilience.

It's the key to ease and joy and contentment.

DESIGNED TO SHINE

You are the peacekeeper of your soul.

You are the conductor of the harmony of your life.

You are the creator of your soulful vision.

You are the designer of the light in your life.

Celebrate your inner light today, my friends. Let it sparkle and shine. Let it glow.

Light up your soul. Light up your world.

There is a ripple effect from every single one of us who wants to make the world a brighter place.

Your beautiful, embodied, empowered, enlightened self is already here. She is just waiting to be more fully illuminated.

You are abundant by birthright.

You are inherently worthy.

You are intrinsically enough.

You are pure light.

You are worthy of being grounded in loving-kindness.

You are worthy of being centered in harmony.

You are worthy of being uplifted by light.

You are designed to shine.

Thank you for being here, in all of your radiance.

I hope you live intentionally to let your inner light shine.

I wish you a love and light-filled life.

PART FOUR

Poems, Affirmations, and Musings from My Heart

DESIGNED TO SHINE

Nature's Applause

Nature's applause:
Can you hear it?
The soft rustling of the wind in the leaves.
The waves of the branches as a gesture of celebration.
The unison of trees celebrating their own beauty with the sound of applause.
The wind picking up, the louder the celebration.
The beauty of it all. Just for us. Just because. Just the existence.
And then they rest. It's part of the process of celebrating.
The beautiful pause in the applause.

Can you hear it?
The soft crash of the waves.
The endless horizon and the gift of the shore as a place to celebrate.
The ocean celebrating its own beauty with the sound of applause.
The wind picks up, the waves pick up, the louder the celebration.
The beauty of it all. Just for us. Just because. Just the existence.
And then it rests.
The beautiful pause in the applause.

Can you hear it?
The soft rhythm of the raindrops.
The clouds nourishing the earth, the plants filled with gratitude.
The water and nature celebrating its own beauty with the sound of applause.
The wind picks up, the raindrops fall faster, the louder the celebration.
The beauty of it all. Just for us. Just because. Just the existence.
And then they rest. And a rainbow appears.
It's part of the process of celebrating.
The beautiful pause in the applause.

PART FOUR

Can you see it?
The light rays, gifts from above, breaking through the clouds, the trees.
The lights twinkling on the top of glass water—angels dancing—celebrating a moment of calm and peace.
The sparkle of a flame, in a candle, in a campfire.
The sparkle of the stars in the sky, the shooting star, the northern lights.
A visual applause of light. Dancing in celebration.
Shining just to shine, just to be beautiful.
The beauty of it all. Just for us. Just because. Just the existence.
Inviting us to take it in. Inviting us to sparkle and shine.
Inviting us to celebrate our light.

Can you hear it?
The love of those around you.
The gratitude for your existence.
A lifetime of hugs and prayers and laughter and tears.
A lifetime of applause.
Allow yourself to hear it.
Allow yourself to receive it.
You deserve it. You are worthy.
Just for being.
Like the trees.
Like the ocean.
Like the rain and the snow and the streams and rivers.
They just exist. And they are beautiful.
Just like you.
All of the universe and all of nature and all of your loved ones
Are sending you applause.
Even when there is the beauty of a pause.
You are a part of nature's applause.

Musings Afterward:

Next time you are out in nature, listen for the sounds of nature's applause.
What is it saying to you?
What can you allow in as acknowledgment?
What should you be applauded for, and can you allow yourself to enjoy the concept that the universe is applauding you right now?
Sit in that energy.
Can you hear it?
Can you feel it?
Can you be with it?
Let it settle in you.

PART FOUR

Aligned in Abundance
I know how to be aligned in abundance.
In an abundance of happiness.
An abundance of deep connections.
An abundance of friends, of community, of love.
An abundance of love.
Abundance is success of the soul.

I know how to be aligned in an abundance of beauty.
In my environment. In my thoughts. In my words.
In my perspective of my world.
I know how to be aligned in an abundance of prosperity.
An abundance of generosity flows through me and back to me.
An abundance of success.
An abundance of knowing.
Abundance is success of the soul.

I know how to be aligned with my inner sage, my inner coach.
To quiet the inner fears, the inner critic, the inner saboteur.
I know how to be aligned in an abundance of peace.
I know how to be aligned in an abundance of harmony.
I know how to be aligned in an abundance of fulfillment.
I know how to be aligned in an abundance of joy.
I know how to be aligned with my inner light.
I just have to choose to allow the alignment.
I just have to choose to allow the abundance.
I just have to choose to be
Aligned in abundance.
Abundance is success of the soul.

DESIGNED TO SHINE

The Beauty of Change

Change is all around us,
Every day, every moment.
In our environment, with our people.

Some of it we welcome and recognize the gifts in the change:
The sound of rain when it's been a while.
The rainbow at the end of a storm.
The gorgeous autumn leaves, first changing colors,
Then falling, raining down in a sunlight sky.
The first snowfall and the beauty of the quiet that comes with it.
The first blooms in spring.
The ice cream cone on summer vacation.

A baby's first laugh, first steps.
A child's first day of school.
These are the easy ones, the joyful ones, the fun ones.

And then there are the changes we have a harder time with, some in a
beautiful way and some in a difficult way . . .
The identity shifts.

They are the big ones.
Graduating college.
Getting a job.
Getting married.
Becoming a parent.

PART FOUR

For some, there is divorce or loss.
A big move, physically, socially, or career-wise.
The move from being called mommy to mom.
The graduations.
The empty-nest stage.
The identity shifts.

We aren't ready, even when we think we are.
It's painful, even when it's great.
And this is the important part to hang on to.
Life is both: the pain and the joy.
It's not supposed to be one or the other.
Embrace the equanimity.

The wrinkles and the gray hair start to peek through.
The reflection changes, and yet the heart remains the same.
There is so much beauty in a life well-lived and a joyous and grateful soul that radiates with those wrinkles and gray hair.
We've met her, we've seen her.
Let's be her.
Embrace the equanimity.

The losses or changes that grieve a future that doesn't get to happen the way you hoped it might.
Life is this series of endless changes.
We can choose to see the beauty in all of it.
The easy beauty, and the difficult beauty.
They can coexist.
Embrace the equanimity.

DESIGNED TO SHINE

Love on your pain of the change.
Love on your identity shift.
Nourish the new version of you.
Nourish the present way things are.
Be here now.
And embrace the equanimity.

PART FOUR

Heart Paintings

Quiet your mind.
Live from your heart.
I know it isn't always an easy road.
Life doesn't just happen to you.
You are life.
You are part of the whole:
The magic and the mystery.

Follow your heart.
Your kind, caring self.
Paint your picture in the universe
And let it paint one back that speaks to your heart.
Dive into that;
Know that your kind heart will always serve you,
Will always lead the way.
Rest when you are weary.
No need to judge.

Connect with that vulnerability.
Give yourself permission to feel your feelings.
Give yourself permission to accept it.
Allow yourself to be curious.
Allow yourself to create more empowering thoughts.
Allow your heart to paint a new picture.

Notice how you meet your days and moments.

DESIGNED TO SHINE

Our heart is always calling us back.
Our heart is where our wisdom lies.
Our heart hears our soul's whispers.
Our heart paints beautiful pictures.
Our heart is home.

PART FOUR

A Part of the Recipe
I see you.
Taking care of your kids.
Taking care of your community.
Taking care of your parents.
Taking care of your job.

You are tired.
You want rest.
But you don't want to miss a moment.
You don't want to fail anyone.
You don't want to be giving less than you should.

Let this be your permission.
Your children need you to rest,
Even if it seems impossible.
Your community needs you to rest,

Even if it seems selfish.
Your parents need you to rest,
Even if they don't realize it or understand it.
Your job needs you to rest,
Even if the demands claim otherwise.

Rest is the gift to your body to be able to show up better and work harder.
Rest is the gift to your mind to be able to think clearly.
Rest is the gift to your soul to find peace and grace.
You need these.
You have permission to give yourself these gifts.

DESIGNED TO SHINE

Everyone who you are taking care of needs you to have these gifts.
It's okay.
Rest.
It's a part of the recipe to be present and not miss a moment.
It's a part of the recipe for success and showing up for others.
It's a part of the recipe for finding calm and still finding the energy to give what you want to give.
It's a part of the recipe for fulfillment.

Take a moment.
Take a pause.
Take a rest.
Let this be your permission.

I see you.
Taking care of your kids.
Taking care of your community.
Taking care of your parents.
Taking care of your job.
Taking care of you.
Well done, my rested and soulful friend.
Well done.
Rest is a part of the recipe.

PART FOUR

Designed to Shine

That inner light.
We know it's there.
We can feel it in our heart.
We can see it in our soul.
And yet...
We don't want to shine it too brightly.
We don't want to speak our truth.
We fear judgment.
We fear annoying others.
We feel unworthy.
We feel unsafe.
And why?
Most of us don't even know why.
It's the mystery of not shining brighter.
At our core,
We believe in our truths.
We believe in our light.
We know that we are designed to shine.
We can feel it in our bones, in our heart, in our soul.
We want to shine our light.
We want to feel seen and loved.
We want to see and love.
We want to radiate that love, that light.
So we decide.
We decide to shine.
We radiate.
We glow.
We are
That inner light.
We are designed to shine.
And so, we shine.

DEDICATION

To my husband and boys: you are the lights of my life. I'm so grateful that we get to be each other's family. I love you with all my heart, always and forever. Thank you for supporting me and my dreams. Thank you for turning the ordinary into extraordinary.

To my extended family, thank you for being the guiding light that shines through the shadows, bringing warmth, love, and hope to all the corners we have traversed together. I love you so much.

To my friends who have been angels and shining stars in my life, thank you for your love, your support, and your patience as I talked about this book for over two years, and the impact you have had on my life. I am so grateful to share this life with you.

To my coaches who helped me overcome self-doubt and make this dream a reality, I thank you for your guidance, and for making me a better coach as well.

To my younger self: great job. We did it.

To God: Thank you for this life. What a light. What a gift. I am eternally grateful.

REFERENCES

Disclaimer: Author is providing examples of studies but is not a scientist or research professional. The author is not in any way claiming or representing an independent confirmation of these studies. The author highly encourages you to do your own research, as these topics have a significant number of published studies that you can readily find and read on your own. These references are provided for informational purposes only.

REFERENCE 1: **Various Studies on Meditation and Potential Health Benefits**

1. Goyal, M., et al. (2014). Meditation programs for psychological stress and well-being: A systematic review and meta-analysis of randomized controlled trials. *JAMA Internal Medicine,* 174(3), 357-368.

2. Hutcherson, C. A., et al. (2008). Loving-kindness meditation increases social connectedness. *Emotion,* 8(5), 720-724.

3. Black, D. S., et al. (2015). Mindfulness meditation and improvement in sleep quality and daytime impairment among older adults with sleep disturbances: A randomized clinical trial. *JAMA Internal Medicine,* 175(4), 494-501.

REFERENCE 2: **A Study on Meditation and Dopamine Release**

1. Kjaer, T. W., Bertelsen, C., Piccini, P., Brooks, D., Alving, J., & Lou, H. C. (2002). Increased dopamine tone during meditation-induced change of consciousness. Cognitive Brain Research, 13(2), 255-259.

REFERENCE 3: **Various Studies on Breathwork Practices and Potential Benefits**

1. Peterson, Christine Tara, et al. "Effects of Shambhavi Mahamudra Kriya, a multicomponent breath-based yogic practice (pranayama), on perceived stress and general well-being." *Journal of Evidence-based Complementary & Alternative Medicine*, 22.4 (2017): 788-797.

2. Aideyan, Babatunde, Gina C. Martin, and Eric T. Beeson. "A practitioner's guide to breathwork in clinical mental health counseling." *Journal of Mental Health Counseling*, 42.1 (2020): 78-94.

3. Chandra, S., Jaiswal, A. K., Singh, R., Jha, D., & Mittal, A. P. (2017). Mental Stress: Neurophysiology and Its Regulation by Sudarshan Kriya Yoga. *International Journal of Yoga*, 10(2), 67–72.

4. Kuppusamy, M., et al. (2017). Immediate effect of Bhramari pranayama on resting cardiovascular variables in healthy adolescents. *The American Journal of Cardiology*, 1(1), 41-46.

REFERENCES

REFERENCE 4: **Various Studies on Gratitude Practices and Potential Benefits**

1. Emmons, R. A., & McCullough, M. E. (2003). Counting blessings versus burdens: An experimental investigation of gratitude and subjective well-being in daily life. *Journal of Personality and Social Psychology,* 84(2), 377-389.

2. Seligman, M. E., Steen, T. A., Park, N., & Peterson, C. (2005). Positive psychology progress: Empirical validation of interventions. *American Psychologist,* 60(5), 410-421.

3. Jackowska, M., Brown, J., Ronaldson, A., & Steptoe, A. (2016). The impact of a brief gratitude intervention on subjective well-being, biology, and sleep. *Journal of Health Psychology,* 21(10), 2207-2217.

4. Wood, A. M., Froh, J. J., & Geraghty, A. W. (2010). Gratitude and well-being: A review and theoretical integration. *Clinical Psychology Review,* 30(7), 890-905.

REFERENCE 5: **Various Studies on Journaling and Emotional Well-Being**

1. Lepore, S. J., & Smyth, J. M. (2002). The writing cure: How expressive writing promotes health and emotional well-being. *American Psychological Association.*

2. Smyth, J. M. (1998). Written emotional expression: Effect sizes, outcome types, and moderating variables. *Journal of Consulting and Clinical Psychology,* 66(1), 174-184.

BOOKS THAT WERE INSTRUMENTAL IN MY PERSONAL DEVELOPMENT JOURNEY AND ARE INFLUENCES ON MY WORK

Buettner, D. (2012). *The Blue Zones: 9 Lessons for Living Longer From the People Who've Lived the Longest.* National Geographic.

Achor, S. (2011). *The Happiness Advantage: The Seven Principles of Positive Psychology That Fuel Success and Performance at Work.* Crown Publishing Group.

Williamson, M. (1992). *A Return to Love: Reflections on the Principles of "A Course in Miracles".* HarperOne.

Seligman, M. E. P. (2011). *Flourish: A Visionary New Understanding of Happiness and Well-being.* Free Press.

Bernstein, G. (2016). *The Universe Has Your Back: Transform Fear to Faith.* Hay House.

Dyer, W. (2004). *Living with Intention: The Science of Using Thoughts to Change Your Life and the World.* Hay House.

Dyer, W. (2007). *Change Your Thoughts, Change Your Life: Living the Wisdom of the Tao.* Hay House.

Made in the USA
Monee, IL
15 December 2023